MW00354115

YOUR CHILD MY STUDENT

Lessons from the Classroom & Beyond

By
Dr. Shekina Farr Moore

Featuring Expert Authors
Lisa W. Beckwith
Marissa Bloedoorn
Shalakee Edwards-Baker
Kelly Gifford
Nina Luchka
Jerry Macon
Dr. Juanita Woodson

Copyright © 2019 by Shekina Farr Moore.

All Rights Reserved Worldwide. Printed in the United Sates of America.

No portion of this book may be copied or reproduced without the written, expressed permission of the publisher, except in the case of brief quotations embodied in critical articles and reviews.

Literacy Moguls books may be purchased for educational, business, or promotional use. For information, please email publishme@literacymoguls.com.

ISBN-13: 978-1-938563-23-2

Published by Literacy Moguls Publishing Co.
www.literacymoguls.com

950 Eagles Landing Pkwy, Ste 610
Stockbridge, GA 30281

FIRST EDITION

Dedication

This book is dedicated to every village member who answers the call to teach and guide our youth and future leaders each and every day.

Table of Contents

INTRODUCTION   **1**

The Importance of Mentorship   6

A Case for Mental Health and Support Services in Schools   22

Leadership Commitment for the IEP Student   78

It Takes a Village   114

Building Confidence in Students   177

When Homeschooling Became My Life   207

The Value of Cultural Sensitivity Training   244

Each One Teach One: Effective Mentoring & Support for New Teachers   262

What Your Kids Won't Tell You   275

Setting Boundaries & Expectations   282

Students' Self-Expression   288

The Expectation of Education   295

MEET THE EXPERTS   **304**

Author Dr. Shekina Farr Moore   305

Author Kelly Gifford   309

Author Jerry L. Macon   311

Author Dr. Juanita Woodson   313

Author Marissa Bloedoorn   316

Author Nina Luchka   319

Author Lisa W. Beckwith   320

Author Shalakee Edwards-Baker   323

REFERENCES   328

"The goal of education is not to increase the amount of knowledge but to create the possibilities for a child to invent and discover, to create men who are capable of doing new things."

-Jean Piaget

Introduction

Your Child My Student, An Anthology

If you know anything about education today, you know that it has definitely changed. Students have changed; parents have changed; and teachers are no longer just responsible or teaching. They have to be everything to everybody—partners with parents and the community, parents to their students (at times), counselors, friends, you name it!

Other New Realities Modern Teachers Faces

> ➢ Designing learning experiences that carry over seamlessly between home and school. So, making "school" disappear and even giving the illusion that you're working yourself out of a job.

> ➢ Troubleshooting technology, including cloud-based issues, log-in info, etc.

> ➢ Verifying student privacy/visibility across scores of monitored and unmonitored social interactions per week; Validate legal issues, copyright information, etc.

> ➢ Refining driving questions and other matters of inquiry on an individual student basis

- ➢ Insisting on quality–of performance, writing, effort, etc.–when the planning, technology, and self-reflection fail
- ➢ Evaluating the effectiveness of learning technology (hardware, software, and implementation of each)
- ➢ Filtering apps based on operating system, cost, complexity, performance, audience, and purpose
- ➢ Clarifying and celebrating learning, understanding, mistakes, progress, creativity, innovation, purpose, and other abstractions of teaching and learning on a moment by moment basis

And this list just scratches the surface of the change in landscape in education. It's a new day and new teachers, parents, youth leaders, and mentors need support in a new way. Hear about their (sometimes) tumultuous journeys in meeting the needs of students.

Your Child My Student features contributors from across the country, and topics include stories from educators' experiences within and outside of schools, barriers to student success, professional and personal growth

"Education is the most powerful weapon which you can use to change the world."
-Neslson Mandela

The Dilemma

The Importance of Mentorship

By Jerry L. Macon

His reputation proceeded him. Unfortunately, his parents were unable to arrest his negative behaviors for any sustained period of time. The worrisome phone calls continued to come at an alarming rate and those calls were causing the ones who loved him most to suffer hardships in their careers and personal lives. No one was sure what his core problems were, but they knew he needed help. An intervention was needed. Real help was required.

Well, fifth grade had arrived for this young man and he had yet to pass a standardized test in math or reading. He'd been advanced along socially so that no teacher had to experience his extreme behavior for more than one school year. Of course, no teacher enjoyed being cursed out, threatened, ignored, disrupted, and dishonored.

The good news for this child, let's call him "Jabez" was his elementary support system. This system included very supportive administrators and lead teachers throughout the building. Jabez, however, frequently exhibited the same behaviors with them, albeit to a lesser degree. Sadly, he still had moments with them that were openly embarrassing and humiliating. So despite all the in building support, nurturing parents and inclusive atmosphere, Jabez continued to rage!

Whether in rage or not, Jabez would harass his fellow classmates and students by demanding his own way, making insulting comments, participating in unsolicited sexual innuendo, and worse yet, he would demonstrate very misogynistic behavior towards women. He seemed to hate the girls in his class and the girls he had conflict with outside of class.

It seemed obvious that his environment was not providing the answers or answer needed for his troubled soul. In fact, his environment seemed to enable his behavior. Enabling is help that will always need to be given. Worst yet, enabling could eventually interfere with true growth and change. Jabez and his behaviors were being tolerated.

To tolerate negative behavior is the beginning of hate. Show me an environment where derogatory behaviors are tolerated and I will show you the beginning of hate. As most teachers would tell you, behaviors are the first thing that need to be in order so that learning can take place at high levels. Order does not mean the absence of nurturing. Order and discipline does not mean the absence of fun. Order and discipline set boundaries for the purposes of safety, security, respect, and learning. These things done with Integrity are safe guides for a quality life.

Jabez had two active, biological parents involved in his life, yet he still experienced difficulties in school. What was going on? How could a mentoring relationship had help in his situation? How does his situation compare to a young lady who grew up in a household led by a single mother? I'll call this young lady Sarah.

Sarah knew of her biological father. As a matter of fact, she had seen him a time or two and knew of his other family. She hid her feelings of rejection by staying close to her mother. Sarah was very proud of her mother, and approached her senior year of high school with great joy. Mom provided a good living. She was excellent at her work and was in a supervisory position. Sarah had no material needs as they were met successfully by her professional, yet available mother.

However, Sarah would hide things from her mother. She hid the fact that she missed her father. She hid the fact that she was angry at him for abandoning them. She hid the fact that she was dating. She hid the fact that she had already had an abortion and was currently pregnant. In fact, Sarah didn't talk to anyone about her pain. Instead, she chose to keep her pain buried and her grades up. She was never a problem at school and was generally well liked by her classmates. She was not without enemies. Many girls in the school were jealous of her beauty and popularity with the boys. They were also jealous of her acceptance as a "good girl" by respected teachers and adults at school. They spread many rumors about Sarah, many of them untrue.

Combined with her new pregnancy, the rumors were getting to her and she started missing school. First a day, then two, then three; finally,

Sarah dropped out before her pregnancy showed to a level she couldn't cover. Although some teachers inquired about her absences, and although she had a senior class counselor, no one reached out to mom the first three months of school. It was a large school that was starting to change over the last couple of years, and negatively due to rezoning. Sarah quietly took advantage of a remote program that let her attend classes away from school and she finished the semester, but during Christmas break, she attempted suicide.

She had earlier seen her father with his new family. They looked happy. Her half-sister seemed secure under her daddy's arms. She was pretty too. She seemed more childlike, more innocent, even though she was just two years younger. Sarah hid herself from them as she began to feel the pain of her father not reaching out for her seventeenth birthday.

She remembered again that he had only left a voicemail for her sweet sixteen and he blamed her mother for his lack of involvement in her life. She told herself she didn't need him, and quietly dated a young man that was ten years older. The same man that impregnated her twice. Sarah was good at hiding things. She survived her suicide with no ill effects. However, her mom was aware of her attempt and was frightened, embarrassed and ashamed. Mom said to herself, "I failed my daughter." She then promptly paid for the abortion.

So what does Jabaz need? What does Sarah need? First and foremost, I believe it to be widely understood that the first relationship of life shaping impact is that of the family. The word family means familiar. There are many ways to become a family. There are many ways to be a family. I'm not here to disqualify family as anyone knows it currently. I'm only here to present irrefutable evidence that can help counter "family gone wrong." Family can go wrong no matter how it is constructed. Whether that construct is traditional (biological parents, in a marriage relationship/nuclear or some other combination, like a family headed by a same sex couple, single mom, single dad, blended families etc. Families can go wrong. They can go wrong from implosion (destruction from within). This means it looks right from the outside, but oh so messed up on the inside, or explosion, meaning the whole world has access to the good, bad and ugly of the family dynamic.

As a parent, gospel minister, teacher, military veteran, public speaker and life coach, I'd like to present a problem that needs a solution. A problem that makes family done wrong unfixable. A problem that leaves no reprieve for familial break down. The problem is a failure to recognize the importance of a healthy, integrity based mentoring relationship, particularly in the absence of these qualities in the parental relationship.

Even the best of parents who raise their children in the best of circumstances, will still have a child influenced by a person or persons other than themselves. Hopefully, that mentoring relationship adds on to the positive quality of their child's development and is not detrimental or harmful in ways that will stunt or regress growth and positive gains of the child. All relationships have a risk factor. Mentoring is no different.

In the case of Jabaz, his parent's seemed to enable his behavior. They meant well, and they undoubtedly love him. However, their son failed to report his observations of his father's verbal, physical and psychological abuse towards his mother. He failed to mention to the people in his life about his mother finding comfort with someone who was treating her right and how she would steal moments with him.

He failed to mention how his mother would cry herself to sleep at night while his father was away days at a time. She needed help. She didn't know where to begin. He needed help, so he would leave to give her a break and to give himself one. They married young and they both had drug addicted parents who were unavailable to truly raise them. They both took the bits and pieces of positive interactions with adults, and ended up having decent careers, or ways to make money. No real investment in time by a caring adult was evident in their formative years. I'd learn about these things through the adult Jabaz, who sought me out and now knew the importance of being mentored. Life had him seek out someone he could trust.

As for Sarah, her hardships brought her out of hiding. Her mom was now in the know concerning her struggles. For so long, mom was doing things on her own. She was prideful and very slow to ask for help. She apologized to her daughter and then admitted she secretly blamed her father for their struggles. Mom confessed her anger towards him, but denied she had any role in his sustained absence. The early years were the toughest.

The missed child support payments hurt. The bills, including those for school were piling up. Sarah's mom was proud of herself because they made it without the consistent support from her deadbeat dad. She wanted her daughter to be proud, too. She did not realize the level of hurt and resentment that her daughter felt. As a gesture of faith, Sarah's mom picked up the phone for the first time in two years to talk with Sarah's dad. He didn't answer.

Mental Health

The Case for Mental Health Support and Services in Schools

By Shalakee Edwards-Baker

Astudent's ability to learn, grow and develop is inhibited when mental illness is undiagnosed or inadequately treated. In today's education system, there exist a lack of mental health support and coordination of services for students, parents and faculty.

National Alliance on Mental Illness (NAMI), a grassroots organization that advocates for mental health services, supports the case that schools need to provide mental health services. According to National Alliance on Mental Illness (NAMI), "mental health conditions usually occurs in adolescence and half of the people living with mental illness experience an onset by the age of 14" (NAMI, 2018). Not to mention that one in five youth live with Mental Illness (MI), but less than half receive the needed services.

"Schools provide a unique opportunity to identify and treat mental health conditions by serving students where they already are" (NAMI, 2018).

Education has always been an integral part of my life. Growing up I can remember one of my first childhood careers as a school teacher. I loved to play school. One summer my cousin helped several of her favorite teachers pack up their classes in preparation for the move to the new Ayden Middle School.

That afternoon when she came back home she had brought lots of the teacher edition books! You know, the one with all the answers. We thought we were certified and I was her assistant. It makes me laugh just thinking about it.

When I was about twelve years old, I cleaned out our upstairs attic and created a schoolhouse. It was during the summer so it was hot, muggy, dusty and not to mention lots of work. But it didn't matter because I simply loved playing school. It was a safe place for me.

You see I lived in a home where drugs and alcohol was present and any day a domestic dispute will ensue between my mom and her boyfriend. We would play school for hours; I was in my happy place but no one could prepare me for what was in store for me as a parent in the real world.

Throughout my high school years, I participated in school activities centered on becoming a teacher in the 21st Century. But due to the salaries for educators in North Carolina I quickly changed career paths. One of my fondest memories in high school was attending a week long summer camp at Fayetteville State University.

During the week long exploration, we had to design a multicultural school for the 21st Century that included diversity and technology. There were about fifty or more upcoming high school seniors that participated from all over North Carolina. We were divided into several groups of about ten to twelve students. In the end, the group that I was assigned to won. I don't remember all the details of the project, but what stuck out to me the most was the slogan, "Preparing Minds for the Change in Times." The logo was a human brain with a ticking clock inside the brain.

Ironically, when mental health is left untreated a person's brain is like a ticking clock with a bomb attached that goes off at any time. One key component of the project that we did not foresee were the challenges of mental health in the education system. This is one reason I wanted to participate in this anthology.
One day this crisis knocked on my front door and the resources and support in the schools

were missing. Professionally, I have worked in healthcare for 25 years so I know how to provide quality care but dealing with a child exhibiting mental illness was new for me. I knew little about mental illness and the effects it has on learning.

My education path changed in 2013 when I graduated with a Bachelor's

Degree in Sociology, with a concentration in Social Problems and Policies. Honestly, I had no intent on pursuing a career in this field but wanted to complete my degree that I was paying for. What I learned most from this program is that there does exist a relationship between experience and the wider society.

This experience was preparing me for something bigger than I.

Background-Detriments to Mental Health

Mental health is defined as, "a state of successful performance of mental function, resulting in productive activities, fulfilling relationships with people and the ability to adapt to change and cope with adversity" (Scheid & Brown, 2009).

As individuals develop, there are certain determinants- a cause of injury or harm, that could potentially affect his/her state of mental health. As we look at the mental health concerns in schools we must understand that there exists certain detriments to mental health. These mental health detriments include race, socioeconomic status, gender and social support.

Race

I'm sure many maybe saying, "boy do I get tired of race being the reason for many of society ills," but we have to be clear and acknowledge that racial ideologies impact our society. A growing amount of evidence demonstrates that racism poses a risk to mental health for minorities.

The higher levels of stigma inflicted on minorities is a chronic stressor that impacts mental wellness (Scheid & Brown, 2009).

Dominant group ideologies such as racism have been in effect for ages and are continuing to negatively impact the mental health of marginal groups. Minorities are expected to conform to the values and standards of the white (dominant) culture, creating an increased vulnerability to depression, anxiety, and substance abuse.

Minorities are less likely to utilize mental health care and have less access to the services. The mental health status of minorities is growing worse - leading to an increase in infant mortality, age adjusted death rates and racial gaps in life expectancy and much more.

Blacks are treated at higher rates in public hospitals for schizophrenia whereas whites are admitted to private hospitals for bipolar related disorders. Cultural factors can increase or decrease the risk of mental health and subsequent treatment. Disparities, availability, accessibility, and quality are burdens that are experienced by minorities as well as individuals of low socioeconomic status (SES).

Surgeon General Satcher stated that there are clear disparities in service and the unmet needs of these people. Major findings in the 1999 mental health report were critiqued in the 2001, *Mental Health: Culture, Race, And Ethnicity, A supplement to the Surgeon*

General Report. It was stated in this publication "that it wasn't so much as to the access of services but once minorities do access mental health care treatment is different. Blacks are less likely to receive counseling and more likely to receive medications; although evidence suggest that blacks prefer psychotherapy and are suspicious of medications" (Scheid & Brown, 2009).

Social Class

Social class, also known as Socioeconomic Status (SES), is determined by several factors: income and wealth, status and prestige which are measured by occupation and education one possesses, and the amount of power an individual possess (Scheid & Brown, 2009).

There is an abundance of data that suggest a correlation between race and SES. These determinants have tremendous implications regarding mental health and the services available. High levels of chronic stress are associated with individuals who are in lower SES. Unemployment and poverty are the major contributors of high levels of stress for this group.

Research makes evident that there is an inverse relationship between SES and a number of mental disorders (Scheid & Brown, 2009.) For example, the highest rates of mental disorders are found in the lower class.

The wealth gap between the rich and the poor is associated with poor health outcomes. More importantly, individuals in the lower class have fewer coping resources, less control over their environment, and "less personal control which wears away at their self-efficacy, success. "SES, is more strongly correlated with psychiatric disorders for whites and they are more likely to be admitted to private hospitals for bipolar disorder" (Scheid & Brown, 2009).

Individuals in lower SES are subject to institutional and individual sources of discrimination. Many scholars argue that "a person's position in society and access to resources result in divergent mental health experiences" (Scheid & Brown, 2009 p.164).

For example, African Americans living in lower social class receive different medicines and care from doctors or medical providers than their white counterparts. Lower working class people have high levels of psychological demands and low degrees of autonomy, or decision latitude.

This results in the increase rates of pill consumption, alcoholism, depression, physical illnesses, and loss of self-esteem that impacts the adults as well as the children in the homes (Scheid & Brown, 2009).

Stress and Social Support

There is a positive relationship between life stress and mental distress. Any environmental, social, or internal demands that causes an individual to change their usual behavior patterns is considered a stressor (Scheid & Brown, 2009).

Life events such as death of a loved one, homelessness, bullying, suicide, social media influencers, school shootings, drug use, anxiety, depression, and increase in youth incarceration are some of the issues youth face.

Stress does not affect everyone in the same way and some social categories are more vulnerable than others. For example, racial minority status or gender may provide individuals with different access to resources and in turn may affect how one responds to stress and illness.

Support can be defined as something that bears the weight of something or gives encouragement and approval to someone or something because you want them to succeed. Social support is an important variable in helping individuals cope with stress and other mental illnesses. It is the perception and actuality that one is cared for. "It is a buffer, a deterrent, and a critical coping resource to dealing with stress. Network ties to family and friend makes up this supporting unit" (Scheid & Brown, 2009). Social support comes in a variety of ways, whether through the degree of emotional actions of love and empathy or structural forms such as money, all are an integral part of support.

Little is known about perceived social support, but it is more important than actual social support. Network ties can also influence a person ability to seek help from professionals whereas, "shame and ignorance are reasons associated with this stigma and not seeking care (Scheid & Brown, 2009).

Funding

The current status of the American economy has impacted the funding for many healthcare programs including mental health. This is affecting the lives of many individuals whom depend on government funded public health care services.

Sadly enough, many end up in jail or prison due to the lack of services and funds available for people dealing with mental health issues. We are living in a time where societal values, professional ideologies and economic priorities are in favor of the wealthy versus the poor. Healthcare is managed and many services once made available to patients suffering from mental illnesses are no longer there. This makes it difficult for the people in low socioeconomic status to receive effective treatment that manages their behaviors.

This poses a great threat to society and increases the crime in schools and many communities already suffering from drugs and gang violence. Many programs are uncertain due to implementation of state budget cuts, managed care and the preference for community treatments.

Our societal structures inclusive of the American government are not committed to ensuring that individuals are cared for. In my opinion this is an act of neglect and lack of government accountability.

This generation of youth are dealing more with advances in technology, social media, depression, bullying, sexual activity, drug and alcohol use, obesity, etc. These are clear signs that a bigger problem exists with school aged children.

Schools are not a mental health treatment center and staff are not trained in this field, but it does provide a more stable and controlled environment to recognize and report signs that may suggest mental health concerns. It is in my opinion and from experience that there is a lack of coordinated services in the schools for youth, parents, faculty, and staff with mental illness. Many leaders in the education department are so far removed from the effects that trauma has on learning that our kids are expected to go back to school a few days to a week after a school shooting. We expect these kids to cope without the necessary support.

Our education system, while moving into another century, must be prepared to include integration of mental health resources and support. In July 2017, our family changed forever. My son was diagnosed with Schizophrenia. It is a complex, long-term medical illness affecting 1% of Americans, and it interferes with a person's ability to think clearly, manage emotions, make decisions and relate to others. The average onset tends to be in late teens to early 20's for men and the late 20's to early 30's for women. It is "uncommon to be diagnosed with this younger than 12 and older than 40" (NAMI, 2018).

Our Story

In the fall of 2014 we made a decision to allow our son to attend high school away from home. Prior to him leaving, he had participated in a summer math tutorial program so that he would be on target for high school academia. He was tested by the tutor to ensure that he was on grade level, and he was. The tutor administered the Scholastic Reading and Math Inventory Test. I remember one evening getting a call from him shortly after school had begun, and he started thanking me for the tutoring. He was confident going into class. That was a great feeling knowing that he recognized it was in his best interest.

Now the school year had ended and he was still away from home for the summer. He had good grades and had been promoted to the 10th grade. On July 11, 2015 around 6am, I got a call from my child. At that time, he had just turned 16; he never calls me at that time. I thought to myself, he wanted to come home. I told him that I had to work, but was off that weekend, and we would come get him. He said, "Ok" and we hung up. That Thursday morning, he called back around the same time, but this time, I could tell in his voice that something wasn't right.

I proceeded to tell him that I'll pick him up on the weekend. Deep down I knew something was going on, so when I arrived at work I called my manager and told her I had to leave. When we first arrived to pick him up, he couldn't be found.

We had traveled from Charlotte, North Carolina to Rocky Mount, North Carolina, which was about a four-hour ride. It was the most awkward feeling I had ever felt. I didn't know where he was or how to contact him because he didn't have a cellular phone. We looked for him for about two hours after arriving in the city and finally found him across the street at my cousin's neighbor house.

That was the first place we went when we first got into town but no one answered the door so we continued to look in places we thought he would go. When he saw us, my husband, his biological father, his sister, brother and me, he had a breakdown.

What happened to my child? Did something traumatic happen? Why did this happen to him? I felt like I had not protected my child. He was innocent, angry, punching things and cussing; which he had never done before, at least not in front of me. He punched the refrigerator so hard that he broke his pinky finger. It took us some time to calm him down before traveling back home.

When we got back to Charlotte, NC, he was taken to the emergency room, treated and released. I told the doctors the aforementioned and no mental illness diagnosis was given so went continued with our normal routines. His primary care doctor was made aware and ordered diagnostic test and psychological test that did not provide any explanation of what was happening.

It was now time to enroll him in school, August 2015, during the fall semester. I had just seen him in May for his 16th birthday and none of these behaviors were present. Nevertheless, we had to remain focused on treatment and getting him back to baseline.

I had so many rummaging thoughts of what could have happened but that wasn't gonna change the current situation, so I had to digress. Upon enrolling him in the Charlotte Mecklenburg School System (CMS), I proceeded to tell the school counselor about the episode previously mentioned, seeking guidance. The counselor listened and proceeded to sign him up for the required classes. But she wasn't listening and didn't provide any advice on what I could do. His grades entering the 10th grade were on target and so they were seeing him based on the previous school year test results and not listening to me.

My child was experiencing a mental health change and no one could have prepared us for what was about to happen.
We sought help from the counselors, scheduled meetings with his teachers and still no help was provided. That September 2015,

he had another episode in uptown Charlotte, while hanging with his friends. He called me and asked me to come pick him up but I said no because he was spending the night with a friend. During our conversation he said, "Bitch we need help." He has never cussed at me or in my presence. It was at that moment I knew he needed inpatient treatment.

My mouth dropped wide open and my heart was broken at the same time. I literally felt my heart rate increase after that conversation. That night he was taken to the Behavioral Health Clinic for Youth. His fourteen-year-old cousin, helped us talk him into getting treatment. It was a success. He was there for two days and was diagnosed with Drug-Induced Psychosis. Apparently, he had been smoking and drinking with his friends. I had no idea that he was smoking "weed." According to the healthcare team, drugs can bring about a psychotic episode.

He had been smoking with his friends. Self-image is important to teenagers, therefore, they want to do everything that the "in crowd" is doing, even if it means to participate in illegal activities such as selling, and usage of drugs. Maybe he was self-medicating, who knows, but this wasn't the child I sent away to school. The doctors prescribed Risperdal as needed to manage his symptoms, but this was all so new.

I must admit, I was still in denial that my son was dealing with a mental health illness.

Although I have years of 25 years in healthcare experience, taking care of a child diagnosed with mental health illness was new to me. I thought to myself, Lord why me? What did I do wrong? Why did this have to happen to my child?

I remember moving him from school to school and place to place. I would beat myself up for allowing him to move around so much. It was my fault, I blamed myself for everything. But regardless of the fact, I would go out to the school seeking support and guidance. We were left in the dark to fumble through the complexities of the system alone.

In the meantime, my family and I would notice continual changes in my son's mood, hygiene, paranoia, staring off, lack of interest in sports, depression, hostility or suspiciousness, extreme reaction to criticism, flat expressionless gazes, inability to concentrate, insomnia, forgetfulness, lack of interest in school performance and being very argumentative.

All of these behaviors were new to me and this was what I considered an "episode". Once we began to educate ourselves, we learned that

symptoms such as hallucinations and

delusions usually start between the ages of 16

and 30. Schizophrenia in teens is difficult to

diagnose and men usually experience

symptoms a little earlier than women (NAMI,

2018).

As time continued to go by no one was

listening, and I continued to fight and advocate,

but the schools were not equipped. The school

system is not equipped with the resources for

students, parents, or educators; resulting in

two years of planning to get help.

I had been advocating for an Individualized Education Plan, (IEP). This is a document created with a team that makes accommodations for a student with learning disabilities and reviewed periodically. The more one knows about the plan the more support can be given to support the academic success of the student. However, I didn't know much about IEP or how it was to be used in helping my child get the best academic support possible.

In July of 2017, our son had another episode and had to be admitted into Behavioral Health Clinic for one month. This admission would come only two months after he turned 18 years old. Again we had to enlist his best friend/cousin's assistance in getting the needed treatment. This time was different and he wasn't coming home in two days. My heart was heavy but with the help of Almighty GOD and my family support it was a little easier to cope with not to mention we had other kids in the home that we had to educate on what was going on with their brother.

Since he was now an adult, things changed and I had to get his permission to access his medical information. He was now in a facility with adults who had mental health illness, and I could not protect him. He was angry and felt like we betrayed him. We had to visit him for a month in this facility, and I cried terribly every day after visitation. I felt like I was leaving him in jail. The only thing that made this better was the fact that my cousin worked at the behavioral center and checked on him daily and he had his co-workers looking out for him as well. So he could see a familiar face daily. To him, he was ok.

I remember him saying at court one day, "all I do is go to school and play sports. I don't get into trouble. Why I am I here?" I was just crying inside and trying to hold it together for him. Nothing was different, so he thought, but things were different and not to mention still trying to get him graduated from high school. We had to attend court in the facility to extend his stay per his health care team. They had wanted to make sure he was therapeutic on his medicine before being released.

He was released from Behavioral Health just a week before his 12th grade year. I really didn't want him to go but this is the last year, so I thought. He had failed a few classes and was still promoted to the 12th grade. The tables turned once he was given a diagnosis of Schizophrenia.

He is under the continuous care of mental health clinician and being managed with medication, Invega Sustenna. This medicine gave me my son back. He was now getting back to his baseline and looking at him or interacting with him was improved. In my opinion, this is when they started to listen, but by now it has been almost two years of seeking educational assistance or accommodations for a child with no success.

He was re-tested by the tutor in September 2017 and the results revealed instead of being on the target grade level with reading and math, he is now on a 2nd grade level. I made sure that I kept the counselor updated on any outside help he was getting. How did this happen? No one provided any help.

The school teachers, counselors, and resource officials are not equipped and trained properly when dealing with mental illness that many youths are experiencing.

In October 2017, we had another meeting on IEP and this time they were listening. By this time, I have met with the school counselors, spoke with his teachers and everyone that would listen to my concerns. It saddened me that his Social Studies teacher voiced in a meeting that he saw my son struggle for a year in his class and didn't mention it or advocate on his behalf.

I now understand that many of our educators and parents have little knowledge on mental health illness and the effects on learning. The impact varies depending on each child and the level of support available. We finally got an IEP in December, 2017. Unfortunately, he went through his 12th grade year and failed several classes.

He had the opportunity to take these classes in summer school to recover the credits but the learning style was not the type needed for successful completion. He was placed at a computer with modules that had to be completed to recover the credits. Well, I guess implementing the IEP in credit recovery was not of importance because it was not used to guide his learning.

Currently, my son is 19 and is repeating the 12th grade. It's been a rough road but just before the start of the 2018 school year we were introduced to another school option.

He is now enrolled in a different school and have the opportunity to play basketball again. Something he couldn't do for the last two years due to poor grades. He was pulled out of the public school system and enrolled in a Charter school with smaller classroom sizes and the faculty and staff seem to be listening to our needs and providing hope.

More importantly is that they take all cellular devices and keep them until school is over. I just loved that. He still has monthly therapist visits, medication management and is on target to graduate in June 2019.

Listed below are signs and symptoms for Schizophrenia obtained from the (NAMI, 2018).

1st Signs-

- Can include change of friends
- Drop in grades
- Sleep problems/irritability
- Isolation
- Unusual thoughts and suspicions
- Hallucinations, hearing voices, seeing things or smelling things others can't perceive. The

hallucinations are very real to the person experiencing it.

- Delusions-false beliefs that don't change
- Negative symptoms-emotionally flat or speaking in a dull disconnected way
- Cannot follow through with activities, show little interest in life or sustain relationships, sometimes these negative symptoms are confused with clinical depression
- Cognitive issues/disorganized thinking, struggling to remember things, organize thoughts or complete tasks.
- Unaware the he/she has the illness

Causes

- Genetics

- Environment

- Brain Chemistry-Neurotransmitters dopamine and glutamate

Substances use- some studies suggest that taking mind altering drugs during teen years and young adulthood can increase the risk of Schizophrenia. A growing body of evidence indicates that smoking marijuana increases the risk of psychotic incidents and risk of ongoing psychotic experiences (NAMI, 2018).

Mental Health Staffing In Schools

The current staffing structure for mental health support in school is overburdened and fragmented. In August 2016, The National Public Radio (NPR), a nonprofit that serves as a national syndicator and provides news and cultural programming, documented in its newsletters that there exists, "A Hidden Crisis Affecting Millions of Students" and the lack of mental health support in schools. Based on that article, schools are in need of more mental health support and services.

The current structure in schools includes: teachers, social workers, school counselors, school nurses, school psychologists, special education teachers, and principals. The problem is that many are overwhelmed and have more students than recommended by the

U.S. Department of Health and Human Services and The Association of School Counselors. The school psychologist should be a key player in intervention and referring of students and parents to outside help. But in the United States, there is only one school psychologist to every 1400 students. The school nurse is also a part of the team that can detect early signs of mental health, however, they have more than 750 students that they are responsible for.

The duties include making sure that immunizations and health records are current and addressing the day to day health needs of the students, just to name a few. The U.S.

Department of Health and Human recommends one nurse to 750 students and is aware of the caseload many school nurses are experiencing. Social workers are also key players in the schools. Truthfully, there just aren't enough social workers in the schools.

One social worker has more than 250 students that they are responsible for and it's no way possible that this is effective in meeting the needs of the students and staff. School counselors have a heavy caseload and in reality they meet the needs of more than 500 students. The American School Counselor Association recommends half the caseload for counselors and their primary tasks include making school schedules and filling out college applications. In my opinion their services should be focused on mental health of students and not school scheduling. The scheduling of classes for a student does not need a Master's Degree or certification. The job description of the school counselors need to be revised to include more mental health support and services to the staff, students, and parents.

The role of special education teachers is to assist students diagnosed with mental health illness in order to help them meet their academic goals. "Nearly every state has reported a shortage and nearly half of all schools or half of all school districts say they have trouble recruiting highly qualified candidates" (Anderson & Cardoza, 2016). The greatest problem based on the article is recruiting qualified teachers. The principal is in charge of the day to day school management operations and what gets priority.

Due to the daily issues that arise priority issues are left on the table until something or someone gets hurt and intervention is needed. Therefore, it's critical to the safety of everyone that we bring awareness and make mental health support and services in schools a "Priority" within the education system.

Preparing Minds for a Change in Times

In order to provide a better social support team and coordination of mental health services in schools it is imperative that measures be implemented for the best interest of the students, parents, and staff. Let me be clear, no I do not think that schools should be taking on this task alone but metal detectors at schools alone is not going to provide a safe and nurturing environment for learning either.

Parents, teachers, other faculty, students, community leaders, faith based organizations and elected officials must get involved and put mental health services and support in schools as a priority. Most assuredly, school personnel play an important role in identifying the early signs of an emergency mental health condition and linking students with effective services and support.

Listed below are recommended suggestions by the National Alliance on Mental Illness so that we can better understand that schools play an important role in identifying the early signs of mental health challenges in kids, and the role we all play in "Preparing Minds for a Change In Times." (NAMI, 2018)

• School systems should collaborate with National Alliance on Mental Illness {NAMI} a grassroots organization that advocates for the services and support that the schools need to provide school with mental health services.

The goal of partnering with NAMI for solutions, will bring programs and trained community mental health professionals into the schools, provide the mental health care or link families to resources in the community.

• School systems could collaborate and partner with local mental health providers in the communities

• Provide more supportive staffing in the class for students that are struggling with consistent behavior issues. Support and help will reduce the confusion and isolation experienced by youth with mental illness conditions and their families.

• Elected government officials and leaders in education, funding is needed to train school faculty and staff on the early warning signs of mental health conditions and how to link students to resources should be increased. "Funding would allow school-based mental health professionals to coordinate services and support between schools and the community mental health systems" (NAMI, 2018).

• Citizens can join NAMI by calling on States and pass legislation that would require school leaders and staff to be trained in the early warning signs of Mental Illness.

• Parents pay attention to changes in your child and educate yourself on mental health illness and notify your child's primary care provider when you notice these changes

• Parents get involved, volunteer at your child's school and work with the faculty and staff not against them

• Parents attend PTA meetings

• Parents set boundaries for your child; children like boundaries,

• Parents know where your child is and the environment he/she is going to when not at home

• Teachers some of the behaviors may not be because the child is "bad" but maybe having issues with focus and attention. They may need classroom modifications to facilitate learning.

• Teachers already have a ton on their plates, testing, lack of resources, lesson planning and grading but if you see red flags "Say something." Don't just have the child constantly removed or suspended from school. These may be signs of impending issues at home or mental health illness.

• Refer to students to school counseling or social worker

• Student education and awareness is KEY and provides students with information on mental health conditions and how to ask for help if they see the signs in themselves or a friend (NAMI.)

There exist a lack of coordinated mental health services and support in schools but we can all make a difference. We must educate ourselves and others and enlist counsel from professionals that provide services to our youth. If you or someone you may know is going through this, they don't have to do it alone. Have them contact NAMI at the following:

CALL THE NAMI HELPLINE 800-950-NAMI info@nami.org M-F, 10 AM - 6 PM ET FIND HELP IN A CRISIS OR TEXT "NAMI" TO 741741

Leadership Commitment for the IEP Student

Understanding How to Individualize Their Needs

By Lisa W. Beckwith

As educators, it is important to understand how to build a rapport and trust with students. We have to learn how to relate to students and what they are not telling us directly. It does not matter if a student is in your general class or has to receive extra support. In order to build a rapport and trust with students, a teacher must develop a connection with students and become a "Popular/Favorite" teacher with them. We all have been students before (and still possibly are). We know what it is like to want your teacher to feel proud about your assignments and if she/he recognizes that you are participating in class.

When a student Listens, Interacts, and is Knowledgeably Engaged Sincerely (L.I.K.E.S) toward a teacher, they will do the work for themselves, but they are also doing it for their "favorite" teacher as well. Their intentions are not to cause any conflicts nor disruption in class.

When a student likes their teacher, they really apply themselves in a way that will show their teacher that they are trying their best. Most of these types of students do not try to cause their teacher any grief or disappointment. As teachers, we make sure that our students are equipped and have all the tools/resources possible in order to make sure their learning is effective.

When this happens, the students automatically feel important because the teacher is giving their full attention to each and every student. Thus, being placed on the "popular/favorite" list from the perspective of the student. Teachers develop relationship with students by simply being transparent, being patient, and showing that they care for their students. Once that is shown, the relationship starts to form between the two. The Golden Rule is to "treat people the way you would want to be treated".

Being respectful is the key to any relationship. The Queen of Soul, Aretha Franklin, had to spell it out for some people to really understand what R.E.S.P.E.C.T is. It is important for both teachers and students to show respect because it somewhat produces their capabilities, potentials, or accomplishments for whatever they are doing.

Teachers set the tone for the classroom, so the respect should originate from their leadership. Teachers never should disrespect students by insulting their efforts and abilities. Nor should teachers provoke students to react in a way that will cause the students to get to a level of frustration because of the words teachers use in class.

Instead, we should exhibit an optimistic approach by confronting students with gentle greeting and inspiring opportunities for success. It is very important for teachers to get to know their student by relating to them, showing compassion of their interests in and out of school, and conveying a genuine care

for their students. Teachers should also
inquire about their students and what their likes
and dislikes are in order to have a well-
rounded relationship with them.

Teachers need to be active listeners and not
just hear what the student is saying. They
should learn how to purposely and genuinely
be there as a sounding board and come up
with solutions to what their students are
sharing with them. Developing a "good will"
connection with students will allow them to feel
liberated enough to share their deepest
emotions.

If teachers connect with students' past teachers, they can sometimes understand what a student may be dealing with without being judgmental toward them.

The key to making a person feel good about themselves is always extending a compliment, as such: "I am noticing that you are putting so much more effort in your work, if you need more help with anything please let me know". Encourage them by saying "You are doing a good job with turning in your assignments". This will build their self-worth.

Applying kindness is the key, because it will shut down any type of negative energy that a student may have toward a teacher. If an issue needs to be addressed as a teacher, students appreciate it more when the teacher pulls them to the side, individually, and finds out what is triggering their reaction. The teacher can find out what is causing them to behave that way.

There are times we have to show "tough love" in a firm, yet fair, manner. Lastly, find out what the students are not telling/sharing with the teacher. It is important to note that teachers should not wait for problems to occur. There are times when students are in a good headspace and they are performing well in class. These are the times to compliment them regarding their work and give them the affirmations that they will need in order to help them grow more fond of their teachers.

Students want to know that their voice matters. We are in the generation where students want to be heard as well as seen. As teachers, we have to be willing to be flexible, and receive feedback from students. It is important to allow students to open up with their ideas, because they just might be able to help the teacher out.

If a student senses that their teacher is a thoughtful individual, then the classroom and environment becomes a more peaceful and happy place. In conclusion, building a rapport and trust with students by relating to them will permit a teacher to connect with the students so they can learn to tell them what they need to know in order to get the results that students need to have in and out of school. Sustaining respectable interaction amongst teachers and students is a versatile and achievable scheme as it nurtures an atmosphere where actual results happen.

How do students deal with IEP teachers?

The most important awareness that new educators should focus on is understanding that being a general teacher could possibly cause you to become a co-teacher as well. It may not be a choice, but instead, it could be a requirement because of the type of students teachers may have in their classroom. A general teacher may have to connect with Individualized Education Programs (IEP) teachers in order to learn how to reach their students.

Having to partner with IEP teachers is a dynamic limitation for both teachers. If everyone is willing to help the student, then it will allow a successful outcome. Build a relationship together and strategize a plan that will give the student the confidence that they will need to feel successful as a student.

The plan will help everyone to stay connected and have effective communication that will cause a stronger learning environment for the students in class and when they have to be pulled for extra assistance. However, this connection has to be developed by the general teacher first.

Several private/charter schools may not have a systematic plan that will meet the needs of most students who need IEP assistant, which could be alarming for the general teacher. They could have a list of students who are below grade level and not even know how to reach them. The benefit of being a co-teacher could be limited, so it is important to ask about the school's IEP program, how effective it is, and how many students are on the IEP roster. In order to have a successful outcome for students, it is important to find out the types of disabilities and needs that the students may have.

The general teacher has to build a relationship with the student and have a relationship that will cause them to carefully consider meeting all needs such as seating assignments based on the student's abilities. The general teacher can set the sitting chart so that students will sit with peers who are on different learning levels, that way, it will cause them to teach and support one another. It will be less intimidating for the IEP students. In general, children want to fit in with the class. Having other students to show them how to solve a problem or understand a concept will decrease the thoughts of feeling less than, and encourage them to understand how to function in class.

Peer support can help students do things that they are not accustomed to doing. For example, higher level learners tend to be note-takers, ask questions and wait to get their answers out. This strategy could possibly help the IEP students see that the teacher allows them to collaborate and strategize with their peers. If students are teaching each other, it is less intimidating. If not, most students with

IEP's deal with feeling uncomfortable and not feeling confident enough to apply themselves in order to understand the subject concepts that are expected of them.

When this happens some students' reactions in class may appears to be defiant and start to exhibit inappropriate behavioral issues. When this happens, it is important for the general teacher to find a way to distract the students by keeping them engaged.

Most teachers do not find out what the student's learning styles are, but once that is discovered, they can find a way to give the IEP a general project-based checklist. When a teacher makes the assignments interesting and hands-on, it can help with a struggling student's desire to do and finish the project.

The goal is not to overwhelm the student with the thoughts of having to finish assignments with no support. The assignment can be a class and home project. If it is a home project, (as a teacher) frequently check-in with the student to make sure they are on track. This type of strategy will help the student to become more interested and focused, and it could help any classroom distractions.

Teachers should work with students to create an effective plan for when things are not well for the student. As general teachers, we are not wanting to excuse students due to their data and levels, however we do want to make sure that the student will get the support that they need.

As the general teacher co-teaches with the IEP teacher, they have to make sure to share information with what is going on in class and to create a system for the IEP student to follow.

For example, the general teacher would make sure that the students will receive the new skills that were taught in their absents. The teacher will stay connected and the IEP teacher could incorporate some of the classroom skills into their work during their session. This should help with their transition process.

Another strategy is when the student completes their assignments, projects, or takeout work from a class, they can earn a reward once they have redeemed the assignments. It will show them that they are accountable for what is expected.

Sometimes IEP students do not have an expectation from the general teacher and is accepted not to succeed just because they are in need of extra support. It is important to find a way to reach a student who does not seem reachable. As a general teacher, always encourage the IEP student to know that they may not be on grade level, however, they have other things to offer in school. For example, it is import for students to still participate in class presentations with others. Help students to feel better about what they can do versus what they cannot do. This will help the student to discover things that they did not identify within themselves.

As the general teacher is building a relationship with their students, they can understand that having a struggle does not mean it will hold them back from classroom experiences. For instance, by nature, we all deal with anxiety issues, a phobia of crowds, a speech impediment, or even ADHD. They should realize that their truth is not something to fear, instead it is something to embrace and learn how to work with.

As educators, we have to realize that the difference between ourselves and students is the fact that we are bigger/more experienced and they are smaller/less experienced. We have to find a way to ensure that these differences do not divide the understanding between the two parties.

When teachers understand that IEP students only need flexibility with time for assignments, they will stop crippling the student with the thoughts of not completing the work. For example, an IEP student does not have to be exempt from assignments, instead they can alter the assignments and when testing, shorten the amount of questions.

We can help the IEP students to break the negative thoughts of being a "bad test" taker. We have to make sure that even though students are below their grade level (and have to complete IEP work study), they are not exempt from grade-level work in the classroom. It will take time, effort, and support on the teacher's part to make sure the student is still introduced to all assignments. This will help the students not to be so far behind, especially for the upcoming school year. Teachers are the key to making sure the students are seeing some grade-level assignments.

One way to do that is to make sure students get background information during class discussions about the topics that are being given week by week. If the IEP students do not understand the concepts, they will not comprehend when the time comes to master the subject (test-taking). In some situations, the teachers can alter the work by giving options such as: drawings, scripts, and strategies for the subject discussed.

Teachers have to find ways to make it easier by shortening assignments, but not ignoring the needs for the student. The goal is to help minimize the student's struggles and learn how to help them master cognitive impairments. Nevertheless, IEP students do struggle with disabilities, and when a general teacher and IEP teacher partner with parents and students, the benefits are unlimited.

The relationship between all teachers can help students to feel good about learning and focus on the things that are difficult for them to handle alone.

Teachers can find tools, resources, and strategies that will mold students a little better and to help them with their struggles. Most students with IEPs truly want their teachers to be there for them. Teachers already know that these students have difficulty in school.

As leaders, we have to ensure IEP students are successful and feel successful in school. Each student has a unique way of learning and it is both the general and IEP teachers who can help them to identify their styles and needs.

Collaboration is very important and it can develop a powerful learning plan that will meet the need for all students. Executing these strategies for teachers and students will help everyone to have an effective school year. What are the teacher's responsibilities for students with disabilities who use accommodations?

The Teacher's Role on the IEP Team

Because teachers often have first-hand knowledge of what works with the student in their classrooms, they are valuable members of the Individualized Education Program (IEP) team—the team that makes decisions about what supports and services a student with disabilities should receive for instruction and testing. In addition to the general education teacher, the IEP team should include the student's parent(s), special education teacher, related service providers (e.g., physical therapist, speech therapist), and, when appropriate, the student him or herself.

These teams should also include an educational professional such as a school psychologist or administrator who is familiar with the state and district learning standards, testing procedures, and policies for implementing accommodations.

Accommodations are reviewed annually during the IEP meeting, or more often if needed. The teacher plays an integral role in this process as the team discusses the student's:

- Present levels of educational performance

- Individual strengths and needs

- Educational goals

Though decisions are individualized to the student and should not be based on a specific disability category, the list below offers some items educators and professionals might discuss during an IEP meeting.

Modalities (e.g., visual, auditory) that work best for the student

- Accommodations that have been tried

- What has worked well

- What has not worked well

- Accommodations that might help the student to access classroom instruction and assessments

- Accommodations that are allowable on state tests

- Who is responsible for assuring that accommodations are available on state assessments as documented in the IEP

- What accommodations the student prefers and what will he or she use

- Challenges of using these accommodations

- The measurements to determine whether the accommodation is working

- Academic or social behaviors that interfere with the student's learning

- Whether the results of classroom assignments and assessments accurately reflect the student's knowledge and skills

After they have chosen the appropriate instructional and assessment accommodations for a student, the team should document both on the IEP form. Although these vary by state, the forms include several sections where accommodations can be specified: communication and AT special considerations, supplemental aids and services, and assessment sections.

Once a teacher begins to provide the accommodations, he or she should monitor whether they are proving effective. Doing so can help determine whether to continue, alter, or discontinue the accommodations. In the event that the accommodations require alteration, the IEP team should meet to document the changes on the student's IEP form.

For Your Information

It is important that a student understand his disability and what accommodations can help him in school. By taking part in IEP meetings, the student can begin to learn to speak up for himself and his own needs.

A student who is involved in the accommodation selection process tends to use the accommodations more often than one who is not involved. Through this process, the student learns to self-advocate and to make important decisions about his needs that he can then apply on the job or when attending post-secondary education.

IEP process

Just because they have behavioral issues does not mean they need a diagnosis.

Myth #1: Every child who struggles is guaranteed an IEP.

Fact:

To qualify for special education services (and an IEP), a student must meet two criteria. First, he must be formally diagnosed as having a disability as defined under the Individuals with Disabilities Education Act (IDEA).

This federal law covers 13 categories of disability, one of which is "specific learning disabilities." Second, the school must determine that a student needs special education services in order to make progress in school and learn the general education curriculum. Not all students with disabilities meet both criteria. Learn more about the process of getting an IEP with our IEP Roadmap.

Myth #2: If something is in the IEP, the school will make it happen.

Fact:

The IEP is a legal contract, so the school is required to provide the services and supports it promises for your child. But teachers and administrators are busy—and human—so sometimes details are overlooked or forgotten.

Part of your role as your child's advocate is to make sure he's getting the services and accommodations outlined in his IEP. Monitor his schoolwork, test scores and attitude toward school. If things seem off track, meet with his teacher to discuss the situation. Explore other ways you can assess whether your child's IEP is being followed.

Myth #3: An IEP will provide services and supports for your child beyond high school.
Fact:

The IEP (and the services it guarantees) will end when the student graduates from high school. Special education doesn't extend to college or the workplace. The IEP team is required to work with the student to create a transition plan as part of his IEP. This plan will focus on the student's future goals and help him prepare for young adulthood.

Myth #4: Having an IEP means your child will be placed in a special education classroom.

Fact:

Federal law requires that children with IEPs be placed in the least restrictive environment. This means students should spend as little time as possible outside the general education classroom. The IEP may specify services and accommodations your child needs to succeed in the general education class. If students spend time in a "resource room" or special education class, that will be listed in the IEP.

Myth #5: The IEP is written by the school, then explained to the parents.

Fact:

According to federal law (IDEA), parents are full and equal members of their child's IEP team. This means that you have a say in how your child's IEP is crafted. Even if you're not an expert on special education, you are an expert when it comes to understanding your child's needs! Your intimate knowledge of your child's development, strengths and challenges, home life and activities outside of school are extremely valuable for developing the IEP.

It Takes A Village

The Case Study & The Perspective

By Marissa Bloedoorn

How have we forgotten such great wisdom, "It Takes a Village to Raise a Child." At no time has it been easy for a parent to raise a child. Every generation has had to face its own challenges and no one can truly say one generation had it easier than the next. The truth can be found in this, ask a parent during a challenging time with their child how difficult it was and no matter the generation that parent will tell you the same, "Its' not easy

being a parent." We missed the plain and

simple rule of "accountability." Accountability of

all parties involved in the raising of a

child starting with the parents, then the child,

then the teacher, and then our communities.

We have talked about the issue but we have

yet to on a large scale make a measureable

impact on the issue successfully. I believe

parents are the critical component to whether

or not their child succeeds in life in becoming a

productive independent adult and positive

contributor to our society or not. I also believe

the child has a critical role in his or

her own success in spite of the parents they

have been given. Lastly, I believe teachers have a priceless opportunity to fill the gap where parents have failed to inspire their children to pick up the baton a secure it in the hands of the child.

It takes a special kind of teacher who is willing to bridge that gap between a parent's lack of knowledge, desire, or ability to inspire their own child. All parties are accountable for the role they play in the final outcome of the child's present and future success.

Parenting Matters and Your Approach to Parenting Makes the Difference

In my book, "Maintain Your Super Hero Status - A Real Parent's Perspective," I take the reader through an in-depth understanding of the role parenting styles have on the outcome of their children. In this book I only have the opportunity to introduce parenting styles and child behavioral outcomes.

The goal is to help you identify which style you currently use so you can determine if your approach has been working or not and if it needs changing. Then to provide you with insight into the best approach based on current research that will get you the results you want to see in your children. I provide a scenario from my own personal experience and identify the challenges, the misguided methods for parenting, the consequences associated with the parenting approach and what can be done differently to start you moving in the right direction.

The key areas I focus on are parenting style, parental involvement, engaging, educating, supporting and holding all parties accountable; parent, child, teacher and community. In this case "community" is focused more on the school administration providing support to parent, child, teacher as they partner together to foster a learning environment that will ensure the child has the opportunity to maximize his or her potential academically and futuristically.

The Power of Partnering: Parent, Child, Teacher, Community

"It Takes a Village to Raise a Child."

- African Proverb

The "Village" benefits from your child's success. The Village consists of the parent, child, teacher, and every member of the community (school, businesses, community based resources, neighbors, family, and friends). How does your child's success benefit the community, you might ask? With the support of the community your child has endless opportunities. Volunteering, playing sports as well as, opportunities to participate in accelerated academic programs. The community benefits in the positive recognition stemming from your child's success and so much more.

Eventually, your child will grow up and most adults that come of age usually remain in their hometown communities. As a result of growing up, dating, getting married, buying a home or renting, successful adults get settled down in their community and begin to give back.

They will share activities, networks, businesses, social connection with neighbors, volunteering to relieve stress and provide for the needy. The list goes on of benefits successful adults bring to their community. The partnership of parent, child, teacher and community bring about positive change situation to situation.

Here's how the partnership can be explained.

1. Parent/Child/Teacher/Community: The Common Goal: To raise a healthy and emotionally well-balanced child who will one day grow-up to become a productive adult that will contribute in a positive way to our society.

2. Parent/Child Parenting Matters: Be intentional, be engaging, be motivating, be involved, and be accountable.

3. Parent/Child/Teacher Teachers are Critical: Keep the faith, be inspiring, be adventurous, be passionate, get refreshed, and remain current.

4. Parent/Child/Teacher/Community: Communities Make the Difference: Be safe, be resourceful, be intriguing, entice curiosity, be interesting, create opportunities, encourage learning, growing, and volunteering, and be supportive.

Parents we are the critical player in this powerful partnership. Our job is to prepare our children for the world; ready to be responsible, teachable, and giving. This means your child is ready to face the challenges responsibility upon entering the classroom. This means your child is ready to learn and show respect to the teacher and others at all times.

This means your child is ready to give back in a positive way to the community in which you live through volunteering. When all of this is in place it proves the undeniable power of partnering; parent, child, teacher, and community.

All parties held accountable to the success of the child by consistently demonstrating the importance of self-awareness, self-worth, self-respect and respect for others, self-leadership, and self-management.

Partnership - Communication – Support – Accountability

I could write to you from the position of a professional in the field of psychology. I can write to you from the position of once being a child, now a parent, grandmother, teacher, or coach. I am all of these! Having over 31 years of direct parenting experience of two entirely different children and a granddaughter with a personality of her own!

The words you read throughout my contribution to this body of work will come from all parts of my whole and my first-hand experience. I am passionate about our young people and concerned for their future if we don't identify parental challenges as well as provide results oriented solutions. Your parenting style will have an impact on your child for the rest of their life.

I recognize the immeasurable value of raising children with a purpose, one filled with great substance and a deep sense of self-awareness and self-worth. The results that come from being an intentional parent vs. unintentional are the successes your child will experience now and well into their future. Parents who understand the concept of self-leadership know it is exactly what a child needs to master as early in life as possible.

Self-leadership is to know who you are, connect with your moral values (personal, family, and society), control of emotions, awareness of your abilities (strengthens and weaknesses), respect for others, and appropriate behavior. These are characters and traits that are cultivated and developed in the home first, reinforced in school, and supported throughout the community (It takes a village!)

Cultivating the Leader within Your Child

As parents it is imperative that we foster an environment in the home that supports the concept of self-worth, self-development, self-awareness, and self-leadership. Ultimately isn't that what we are doing raising our children to lead themselves and possibly one day become a leader of others.

Our children must first master self-leadership and when they come into the fullness of what it means they can then become successful leaders of others. If an individual has no desire for self-awareness that individual lacks any sense of self-worth. Harvard Business Review argues that leaders who lack self-awareness and a desire for self-development will not strive to learn more or maximize their potential.

I would argue "individuals" who lack a sense of self-worth will not strive to learn more or maximize their potential in life.
Parents, this is the role we play in making a powerful mark on our children that no challenge in the world can erase. I look at it this way, the first relationship a child has is with his or her parents.

It is the foundation of the parent/child relationship that sets the tone for all other relationships.

It's like building any structure the most important part in the building process is the foundation. If the foundation is laid right you can huff and puff until the world freezes over the building is not coming down. Why?

Because the foundation it was built on was properly laid which made it is unshakable. That's what we need to do as parents, lay down for our children an indestructible foundation so that when all hell breaks loose they know how to independently stand and come out stronger than ever before.

Case Study: Every Family has Its Challenges

If it's okay, I would like to share my story. The Case Study is of a family member I had access to since I was a child. I was able to observe from very early on the subjects involved in this situation. I have knowledge of the details and most of the occurrences that lead to the present day outcome.

This is not easy for me to share but it's the truth and it's worth the cost that comes from being transparent. I have shared in my published work the story of my childhood and my journey growing up with parents who loved me but were uninvolved parents. Had my parents been just a little bit more involved and intentional it is my belief that things would have turned out very differently for me.

Because I have shared my story in other books, this time I want to share what I observed in other parts of my family. As a child I didn't know any better we were having fun and enjoying life.

My mother was a woman of tradition. Holidays were always festive at our house. Our family would always find their way to my momma's house during the holidays.
Our home was the place to be for family to come, meet, and feel right at home. As I got

older I began to see our family flaws. In my family parenting was far from intentional as much as it was all about love, affection, rules, boundaries, and responsibilities. The focus was on the here and now not planning for a tomorrow or thinking futuristically at all.

The discussion of post-high school education was not a dinner conversation nor were there any real conversations about career options at all. I worked while in high school not because my mother ever told me to get a job. My friend's mothers told them to get jobs and so I got a job too. That experience influenced my independence. I wanted to work and make my own money. As much as I had drive and ambition that was not being taught nor discussed in my house.

As a parent it is imperative that you engage in dialogue with your children regarding such critical conversations that will shape their future. Had my parents engaged me in such conversations I would have been better prepared for strategizing on my own to create the future I wanted.

I get it families are facing financial challenges, keeping a roof over your family's head, clothes on your back and food on the table are top priority. That's even the more reason to have such critical conversations. If we want our children to do better we have to show them how to do better. It becomes a double-edged sword that teaches in both directions educating the parent as well as the child. You learn to do better as you teach your children how to do better.

It starts with a simple conversation that introduces your child to the importance of self-leadership, self-awareness, self-determination, self-confidence with the goal of building a strong sense of self-worth and a desire for self-development. As a result of my family's lack of being intentional, having those guiding conversations, and thinking futuristically today we have a great deal of dysfunction across four-generations.

We have a great-grandmother in our family raising her great-grandchildren, her grandchildren live with her and her children have low paying jobs barely getting by. This did not have to be the case at all.

Just a slight adjustment in their approach to parenting the elders in my family would have taken their children to a level of continued success and today this great-grandmother could have been relaxing, traveling, and enjoying her full-retirement. Instead she is struggling to make ends-meet and laboring like a young mother with the reality of an aged body unable to keep up.

Teaching our children self-worth and self-determination are important factors to mastering self-leadership with the underlying goal of maximizing your child's potential for achieving and living a fulfilling life. Parents must become cognizant of their approach to parenting, why they do the things they do and the life-long impact their approach has on their child.

Parenting: The Impact and the Results

Back to the case at hand! How did this happen? How did this once-mother-now-great-grandmother become the caregiver for three generations of offspring back-to-back? It happened when this great-grandmother first became a mother. For whatever reason instead of being involved in her children's lives, she focused her energy on providing for them. Provide for them she did and very well! I watched throughout the years her two children want for nothing. Christmas at their house was huge.

The children always had the latest and greatest toys. Yet, they were classified in school, performed below average and stayed in trouble as they got older. The daughter would eventually become pregnant with her first child during her adolescent years. In the years to follow she would have three more children which would all be raised by her mother. Her children would have children and they are now being raised by her mother. This 70-year old great-grandmother has been raising children from birth to adulthood for three generations.

Unfortunately, she brought this on herself. She didn't realize what she was doing at the time, in her mind she was providing for her children. Perhaps her motivation was based on her own childhood, what she didn't get when she was growing up. As a result of her approach to parenting she raised dysfunctional and dependent adult children. Failing to recognize her not so good approach to parenting she went on to raise her grandchildren to be semi-dependent adults.

At some point we have to recognize the impact we are making on the lives of our children. We want them to have a true sense of self-worth and self-accomplishment that can only come from being raised by parents who are intentionally involved in the life of their children.

To understand, correct, or improve your current approach to parenting you may have to look at your childhood to see why you're parenting a certain way. I know I did. I had to take a hard cold look at my past, my family, the dynamics of our relationships starting with the relationship I had with my mother and father.

Now at this point my 70-year old family member has come to terms with her choices as parent and shares with me often. Regardless of where you are today in your parenting approach you have the opportunity to change it once you recognize where we are missing it and are willing to make the necessary changes in your behavior to ensure your children are healthy, happy, and whole.

The Case Study: What happened in this case and how can we do better?

This great-grandmother had a few challenges to her parenting approach which many parents make the same mistakes some knowingly but most unknowingly:

These are critical to fostering a strong sense of self-confidence and self-worth for a child:

1. Lack of Intention – she didn't have it to give to encourage purpose or value

2. Critical Involvement – gifts over quality of time children prefer your time and care.

3. Avoidance – she worked instead of parenting, work was easier to deal with

4. Communication – was usually harsh and demeaning destroying self-esteem

5. Consequences – too harsh and didn't match the crime it was based on emotions

As result of this approach the great-grandmother had to raise three generations of children. Her direct offspring were classified in school, had good character but poor moral judgment, challenges with the law, and low to no income.

Let's take a look at her approach. You could say her approach was a combination of authoritarian, permissive, and passive. In the next chapter we will review parenting styles, child behavioral outcomes and the lifetime impact on the success of the child based on parenting styles.

In addition I will provide resources that can help you become a great communicator with your child, learn how to engage your child in gaining purpose in life, the importance of family traditions in fostering self-worth and value, how to support your child's development process and how to hold your child accountable for their life present and future.

Yesterday's Challenges to Parent are Now Combined with Today's Challenges

I don't believe the challenges of yesterday for parents has disappeared I believe they are now compounded with today's issues. I remember when I was growing up the challenges for parents were; medical care, food, appropriate clothing, and standing up straight.

Today parents are challenged in these areas; belief in self, confidence and capability, stress and crisis, self-awareness (strengths vs. limitations), feeling safe, secure and loved (The Center for Parenting Education 2018).

Yesterday's parents dealt with basic needs while today it is all about emotional needs. Children now require a high level of attention and care from their parents. Today many parents are dealing with all of it, yesterday's challenges as well as today's challenges.

The measurement in the past for good parenting was judged based on whether or not your kids were dressed appropriately, they behave in public, and they are within reason well taken care of. Today good parenting is measured by how well balanced your child is emotionally; is your child confident, capable, have self-value, secure, loved, manages stress well, and self-aware.

The focus on emotions is a clear indicator that our children are dealing with self-esteem issues. Self-esteem and self-confidence are secured by your parents from the very start of a child's life!

This is the very foundation I mentioned earlier in the text. When a child feels loved and valued at home they don't need the world to validate them. Now let's couple a child feel loved with a child knowing the options he or she has to explore and discover the world around them.

Now that child has great possibilities of making a remarkable impact on the world around them. Parents you never know who you're raising up until you watch their lives unfold in front of you.

I'm pretty sure Martin Luther King, Sr. and Alberta Williams King had no idea they would bring into the world the greatest Civil Rights Leader in the world! Harriet Greene and Ben Gross had no idea their baby girl born a slave would become an American abolitionist and political activist.

Harriet Tubman is known for her bravery as a conductor in the Underground Railroad risking her life to free enslaved people, family and friends. Putlibai Gandhi and Karamchand Gandhi were clueless their son Mahatma Gandhi would lead India to its independence and inspired movements for civil rights and freedom around the world using a non-violent civil approach to disobedience.

Parents we have no idea the potential God has placed in our children that is why it is imperative that we strive to do our best to cultivate in our children a desire to be and do great things starting with good character, moral values, and self-worth. Raising children to be emotionally sound and thrive in the world is the top priority for most parents.

Successful parents work hard and raise their children with intent. Some common factors parents who raise successful children are parenting style, they take their children everywhere with them, play traditional board and card games, get in route exercise, and they eat together as a family.

Our role as parents our child's education and life-long success is to create in them a hunger for knowledge! Make them teacher ready. Help teachers educate your children by becoming a proactive partner. Be on a mission to provide your child(ren) with the best opportunity possible for them to excel in learning and development.

Baumrind's Parenting Styles

In 1966 researcher and psychologist Diana Baumrind established a parenting model which consisted of three initial styles of parenting. Maccoby and Martin (1983) later expanded upon Baumrind's work and added the uninvolved/neglectful style.

The authoritative parenting style is more balanced in which there is reasoning that takes place between parent and child. In this scenario there are boundaries set that are reasonable and understood by the child because the parent has explained them. The authoritative approach or parenting style is considered to be the best approach because of the level of balance in controls and freedoms.

The permissive parenting style is very involved with the child, providing a loving environment filled with affection. This is another form of extreme in which the parent is afraid to discipline the child for fear of losing the relationship. In this situation the parent always gives into the child's demand and the child wins.

The authoritarian is like a dictator, has a need for a high level of control with low acceptance, often referred to as the "army style." This style parenting there is one-way communication in which the child is told what to do and expected to follow every command. Discipline is systematic with the intent of maintaining control.

The last parenting style is the passive or neglectful which is low in nurturing, communicating, expectations, and control. In this scenario the parent is disconnecting emotionally and in some cases physically. The objective of this parent is to merely provide the basic needs of the child such as food, clothing, and shelter.

The results or effects of these parenting approaches can be found in the behavior of the children. Authoritarian parents have children who are most likely to be unsociable, unfriendly, and withdrawn (Baumrind, 1971).

Permissive parents have children who are

most likely to be immature, moody, dependent,

and lack self-control (Baumrind, 1971).

Authoritative parents are likely to have children

that exert good social skills, liable, self-reliant,

and independent. And, finally, uninvolved

parents are likely to have children who are

indifferent and have rejecting behavior

(Baumrind, 1971).

Behavioral Outcomes Based on Parenting Style

Effects of Parenting Styles on Children Behavioral Outcomes				
Effects →	Self-Image	Emotions	Social Skills	Academics
Authoritative	High self-esteem Assertive	Trust feelings Regulate well Self-control	Socially responsible Less peer pressure Get along Empathetic	Learn well More confident High achievement
Permissive	High self-esteem Self-confident Less responsible Impulsive	Irregular Voice feelings	Trouble keeping friends	Low interest in school
Authoritarian	Low self-esteem	Don't trust feelings Weak behavior	Don't get along Poor social skills	Hard to concentrate Mid achievement
Uninvolved	Low self-esteem Little confidence Hates self/others	Hide feelings Irregular feelings Avoid feelings	Withdrawn Disrespectful Distrustful	Perform poorly on their own

This chart is a general summary of the effects of each parenting style: how the child see's themselves (esteem), feels, acts in society, and succeeds in education.

Assessing Your Parenting Style

Offered by Psych Central – The Parenting Style Quiz is a tool is used in this book to identify your parenting style and provide an in-depth understanding of your personal style based the four parenting styles discussed in this chapter. Parenting Quiz website:

https://psychcentral.com/quizzes/parenting-style-quiz/

Instructions: This quiz is designed to help you better understand your parenting style. For each item in the quiz simply indicate how much you agree or disagree.

This takes most people about 4 minutes to complete. Take your time and answer truthfully for the most accurate results. If both parents are available, they should both take the quiz and then compare their parenting styles. To understand these results we must ask some serious questions and be willing as parents to take a good long hard look at ourselves. Once we have taken that look we must then take necessary steps to change some things.

Parenting must be a selfless partnership with your children in order for them to become the person that God intended them to be with minimal damage or straying from the originally orchestrated path. To evaluate these four parenting styles and the results there are two indicators communication and warmth and nurturance determine the level of acceptance parents demonstrate with his or her child (Parentastic.org).

Are you listening to your child, adolescent, or young adult? How are the paths of communication with your child; are they one way, reciprocal, or transactional?

Nurturing your child requires you to be reassuring, warming and welcoming during times of need, showing attributes of genuine concern and care. Do you provide this type of environment for your children?

My purpose in contributing to this project is to cause us as parents to think more deeply into the role we parent(s) play and the life-time impact our parenting style has on the children we raise. Here are 12 ways to become a more authoritative parent.

12 Ways to Become a More Authoritative Parent

1. Listen to Your Child

2. Offer Incentives

3. Validate Your Child's Emotion

4. Let Your Child Make Minor Choices

5. Consider Your Child's Feelings

6. Balance Freedom with Responsibility

7. Establish Clear Rules

8. Turn Mistakes into Learning Opportunities

9. Offer One Warning for Minor Issues

10. Encourage Self-Discipline

11. Use Consequences to Teach Life Lessons

12. Maintain a Healthy Relationship

WHY is this ALL so Important?

1. Why is it important to *listen attentively to your child*? By taking time to listen to your child you validate their self-worth.

2. Why is it important to *validate your child's emotions*? By validating your child's emotions it lets them know you care and have empathy for them.

3. Why is it important to *consider your child's feelings*? By showing your child their opinion counts and should be considered by others.

4. Why is it important to *establish clear rules*? By establishing clear rules it teaches your child the importance of boundaries, what is appropriate and what is not. It lays the foundation for setting and honoring boundaries in all relationships and to honor the rules in all situations.

5. Why is it important to *offer one warning for minor issues*? By offering one warning for minor issues it sets the standard for your child to be obedient the first time.

6. Why is it important to *use consequences to teach life lessons*? By using consequences to teach life lessons you teach your child to think critical. Life lessons are more memorable and act as a total recall when the same situations present itself your child will remember and make wiser decisions.

7. Why is it important to *offer incentives*? By offering your child incentives it motivates them to set and achieve goals because they know they will receive a reward when they do.

8. Why is it important to *let your child make minor choices*? By giving your child the opportunity to make choices it teaches them how to make decisions independently and develops their self-confidence, self-esteem, self-awareness, and self-leadership.

9. Why is it important to *balance freedom with responsibility*? By balancing freedom with responsibility you are teaching your child self-management and self-discipline. Having freedom provides your child with the opportunity to become independent. Freedoms are

granted gradually based on the level of development and maturity.

10. Why is it important to *turn mistakes into learning opportunities*? By turning mistakes into learning opportunities you teach your child that perfection is not reality and that we all learn from our mistakes. Mistakes are inevitable and are going to happen. By having a healthy conversation with your child you protect their self-esteem and self-worth. Don't minimize the mistake but don't make it extreme either. Be claim, reasonable, and fair in your discussion.

11. Why is it important to *encourage self-discipline*? It is important to encourage self-discipline to teach your child self-motivation, self-determination, drive and ambition to succeed in life. You don't want to spend the rest of your life telling your child what to do and when he or she should do it. You want them to be responsibility for themselves as they grow into productive adults and have self-accountability.

12. Why is it important to *maintain a healthy relationship*? It is important to maintain a healthy relationship because your child needs you more than you will ever

know. Your child may never tell you just how much they need you in their lives and no matter what they have done or you have done to them the relationship cannot be breached. Your child's self-worth, self-esteem, self-confidence, good character and moral integrity are all wrapped up in their relationship with you. If your relationship is broken it may break your child and destroy their self-esteem. As a parent we never want that to happen.

These are 12 ways to transition from your current approach to parenting to a more authoritative approach to parenting. Keep in mind your children are people too, which have feelings, emotions, their own desires and wants, they need you to love them and to guide them as they grow into their own identity and mature. Beyond your love and affection your child wants to feel they have their own place in the world they want to be valued, heard, and respected just like you when you were a kid!

5 Characteristics and Behaviors of Successful Parents

Start to enjoy your parenting experience and remember your children are a priceless gift. You will only have your children under your wing for a short period of time before they take flight on their own. You want to do everything in your power to make sure they are ready for takeoff and have the skills to maintain throughout their lives a smooth flight with a successful landing.

Here are 5 Characteristics and Behaviors of Successful Parents.

It's time to start enjoying your children…

1. Parents with rules they enforce using a warm nurturing approach with rationale to support their expectations gain and maintain respect and cooperation throughout their parenting experience (Journal of Adolescence, 2012)

2. Take your children with you, stop leaving them behind. You will benefit from the sacrifice more than you know in the future. Travel helps kids grow and mature the frontal lobe the area of the brain that processes cognitive functioning, social intelligence, attention, motivation, memory and more (The Telegraph, 2017)

3. Play more with your children. Did you know that card games improve math skills, memory and strategic thinking (Wall Street Journal, 2015)?

4. Fathers get fit! Did you know men who exercise increase the learning and brain function of their offspring (Cell Reports, 2018)

5. They say a family that prays together stays together! A family the eats together are healthier and happier (American College of Pediatricians, 2018).

Statistically Speaking:

- Two-thirds of conversations between parent and child are focus on daily activities.

- 65 percent of parents admit to only playing with their children occasionally.

- One out of six fathers stated they don't know how to play with their children and another third said they just don't have the time to play with their children.

- Only 25 percent of children stated they talk to their parents once a week about something important to them.

- Research shows the link between relationship health and physical health is vital therefore families need to pay better attention to relationship health to maintain physical health. (Telegraph, 2017)

What are these stats saying parents? We need to strengthen the relationships we have with our children. No more getting mad at your child for failing to meet your standards.

You need to make sure you build a strong loving, supportive, uplifting, and mutually respectful relationship with your children. I witness parents speak so demeaning to their children and this is all ages as small toddlers to teens and even their adult children. My heart breaks!

Our children did not ask to come into this world and whatever choices we made are our own doing, not theirs. They deserve the best opportunity you as their parent can offer! This is not about you this is about equipping and empowering our children to achieve great monuments of success!

Recommended Reading for Parents and Teachers:

For Parents:

- Maintain Your Super Hero Status, A Real Parent's Perspective by Marissa L. Bloedoorn, M.Sc, DTM. https://www.tcsconsultingllc.com/

- The Turnaround: Parenting Tips for Improving Your Child's Academic Success, How to Make Your Child Smarter, Learning-Ready, and Nonviolent by Deborah L. Kelly, Med, CPE.https://www.amazon.com/Turnaround-Parenting-Improving-Learning-Ready-Nonviolent/dp/1500852120

- What Children Need to Be Happy, Confident and Successful: Step-by-Step Positive Psychology of Help Children Flourish by Jeni Hopper - https://www.jkp.com/uk/what-children-need-to-be-happy-confident-and-successful-2.html

Other Reading Resources:

- Ginsburg, K., & Jablow, M. (2014). *Building resilience in children and teens: Giving kids roots and wings* (3rd ed.). Elk Grove Village, IL: American Academy of Pediatrics.

- Morrison, M. (2007). *Using humor to maximize learning the links between positive emotions and education.* Lanham, Md.: Rowman & Littlefield Education.

- Strider, Mac. "What's Your Parenting Style | Parenting Tips For Raising Successful Kids | BetterParenting.com. N.p., n.d. Web. 25 Mar. 2013.

For Teachers:

- Crone, D., Hawken, L. S., Horner, R. (2015). *Building Positive Behavior Support Systems in Schools, Second Edition: Functional Behavioral Assessment* (2nd ed.). New York: Guilford Press.

- David, D., & Sheth, S. (2009). *Mindful teaching & teaching mindfulness: A guide for anyone who teaches anything.* Somerville MA: Wisdom Publications.

- Nelson, J., Lott, L., & Glenn, S. (2000). *Positive Discipline in the Classroom: Developing Mutual Respect, Cooperation, and Responsibility in Your Classroom.* Harmony.

- Nelson, J., Escobar, L., Ortolano, K., Duffy, R., & Owen-Sohocki, D. (2001). *Positive Discipline: A Teacher's A-Z Guide, Revised 2nd Edition: Hundreds of Solutions for Every Possible Classroom Behavior Problem (2nd ed.).* Harmony.

Chapter References

Anderson, J., and Trumbull, D., (2014). American College of Pediatricians. The benefits of the family table. Retrieved: https://www.acpeds.org/the-college-speaks/position-statements/parenting-issues/the-benefits-of-the-family-table

Baumrind D. (1991) The influence of parenting style on adolescent competence and substance use, The Journal of Early Adolescence, Vol. 11, No.1, pp. 56-95

Benito, E., C. Dean, Edbauer, D., Fischer, A., Ramachandran, B. (2018). Cell Reports. RNA-Dependent Intergenerational Inheritance of Enhanced Synaptic Plasticity after Environmental Enrichment. 23, 546-554. https://doi.org/10.1016/j.celrep.2018.03.059.

Shellenbarger, S. (2015). The Wall Street Journal. Management & Careers. How family card games teach math, memory, and self-confidence. Retreived: https://www.wsj.com/articles/benefits-of-a-family-card-game-1428444818

Sunderland, M, Dr. (2017). The Telegraph. The science behind how holidays make your child happier and smarter. Retrieved: https://www.telegraph.co.uk/travel/family-holidays/the-science-behind-how-holidays-make-your-child-happier-and-smarter/

Van Gundy, K., Trinkner, R., Rebellon, J., Cohn, E. S., Cesar, J. R., (2012) Journal of Adolescence. Don't trust anyone over 30: Parental legitimacy as a mediator between parenting style and changes in delinquent behavior over time. University of New Hampshire, Durham NH. 35, 1(119-132). https://doi.org/10.1016/j.adolescence.2011.05.003

Wagenhals, D., (2018). Center for Parenting Education Organization. Why is it so hard to parent today? Retrieved: https://centerforparentingeducation.org/library-of-articles/focus-parents/hard-parent-today-big-picture-parental-responsibility/

Building Confidence in Students

By Kelly Gifford

I started teaching dance when I was 16 years old. To be honest, my motivation at that time was simply to make some money, but very quickly I realized that it was so much more than that for me.

As much as I was giving to my students, I was receiving double. I didn't know then the kind of impact teaching would have on my life or how fulfilled I would feel. I had no clue that I was going to be able to share a gift with my students nor did I realize the impact it would have on them. I danced at a very prestigious dance school in my hometown. It was THE place to dance. I did not begin as a dancer. I was a gymnast.

I was registered at the gymnastics club next door to the dance school and I would go in to this dance studio every single week after my class to watch the ballerinas. It was love at first sight. My parents registered me for my first class the following fall. I loved everything about that jazz class.

I loved my gorgeous teacher, who had long beautiful black hair that she wore pulled back in a tight ponytail, with stunning big eyes and red lipstick. She was so nice, so encouraging. I couldn't wait to get to class each week. She left mid-way through the season but I will never forget how she made me feel when I was in her class.

It was the perfect first experience in dance. I was asked to go competitive the following season. My dreams as a nine-year old were coming true. Little did I know, that this was going to be the beginning of years of tears, shame, pain and feelings of worthlessness.

My new teacher was tough. She was very demanding of me being my best at all times and for this I have the utmost respect for her.

However, it was her constantly breaking me down that had the most damaging effects. I don't really remember anything too negative at 10 and 11 years old but from 12 years on, when I cared more than I should about being liked, and being perfect, and being important was when I suffered the most. She would at times call me names, jokingly, but what child really understands sarcasm?

She would remind me often that I would never be a dancer. She told me I must lose weight (5 lbs) in order to stay on the competitive team, or my favourite tactic, (Yes! There was a little sarcasm in that) the compliments that were embedded in an attack like "thank goodness you are such a great tap dancer because you are not flexible".

These comments that probably rolled off her as tough love and not that big a deal, were crippling to me. I lost the 5 lbs but was terrified to gain it back so I lost another 5 just in case and I was paraded around the studio under her arm while she told all of the other girls how proud she was of me because I looked so good...Yes, you saw that one coming a mile away...that was the beginning of my long battle with disordered eating.

It was the beginning of panic attacks, and a burning desire to please in any way possible. Even with all of the accolades I received as a dancer at competitions, I never believed I was good enough because I didn't have her approval. The story begins to change for me at sixteen years of age.

I had an opportunity to apply for a teaching position with our local community center. I was thrilled when I got the job. I was going to instruct 3 dance classes once a week.

It was a massive learning curve for me. That first week I struggled with those classes of 4 year olds. I had no clue how to teach them and they ruled the room for the entire, grueling and very long 30 minutes. I knew I had to act quickly if I was going to be able to do a great job.

I am a perfectionist and I need to be the best at anything that I do. Which can be a blessing and a curse. I needed that money and I wanted to keep that job. So, I researched and asked to watch classes at my studio with other teachers that were teaching the same age. I put together a program and went back the following week armed and ready and it worked!

They loved the class! I was getting hugs at the end of the class, drawn pictures in the weeks to follow, parents sharing how much their child was enjoying the class, and that just pushed me to be better each class.

Fast-forward a few weeks and my supervisor comes in to view the classes and do an evaluation of my teaching. I was a mess. Stressed to the max that I wasn't going to be good enough. She phoned me the next day to tell me how impressed she was and to offer me more classes in the next session. Over the next two years, I was offered more and more classes from her until I was basically running the entire dance program within the community center. Classes were always full and I had an amazing reputation.

She helped me every step of the way, coaching me, supporting me, validating me and complimenting me when it was due. I was on cloud nine and I was feeling so successful. I was still dancing and competing during the time that I started teaching. I was volunteering a lot at my studio assisting in classes.

My teacher arranged a mentor program where the senior dancers were paired up with one or two of the younger dancers and we would run their solos and help them. Many of my class mates did the bare minimum with the mentoring and soon I was begin asked by other kids if I could help them too. We were supposed to have one or two kids and I ended up with twelve. These were the kids at the studio that my teacher had no use for because they weren't "gifted" dancers.

All I saw were their hearts and their love and their passion and I could connect with their desire to be better and to be recognized and validated. So I did just that. I celebrated their successes individually, I complimented them, gave them my attention, I was just doing what I felt was right in my heart. I was just being me and I really loved it. I didn't really notice until much later on that this was my gift. Things slowed down for me as a dancer a bit due to an injury in which I have to take a full season off of dance but I did continue competing until I was 17 and taking classes until I was 18.

During my last year at my studio, one of the teachers moved out of province and the studio owner was desperate for a teacher. She asked me if I would like to take over the classes for the remainder of the year. So now you are saying, well Kelly, if she didn't like you that much then why would she offer you this position?

Here's why, they were musical theatre classes. I was an actor and she was desperate. A lot of students had dropped this class prior to me taking over and I asked the studio director (my teacher) if she would mind if I contacted all of the students who had previously dropped the class and offer them a free class with the new teacher?

She said sure. So, I sat on the phone (because this was before emails) and invited all of the kids back. Well, it worked! Every single one of the kids that had dropped out returned to the class for the remainder of the year and I was feeling pretty fantastic.

I was proving my worth to her and I knew that this would be the moment I had dreamed about for years. At the end of the season she handed me a card and gave me a hug. It was so awkward for me because I was convinced she hated me. She said to me "When I hired you I was desperate. I needed someone to teach those classes and I figured you were my only option.

I have to say I am pleasantly surprised. If anyone said to me two years ago that Kelly Gifford would be teaching for me I would have laughed in his or her face" She made that comment to me 25 year ago and I can remember it word for word. I will never get those words out of my head. It was the most backhanded compliment you could ever receive but it was that comment that made me realize in that moment that I was going to be a teacher for the rest of my life. That I was going to impact youth for the rest of my life and that I was NEVER ever going to make a student feel the way she made me feel. I was determined to make her eat her words.

I was hired again the next year (and for 10 years after that until I opened my own school). The next fall I turned 19 and was accepted into a performing arts college to begin my studies. It was like nothing I had ever experienced before. My teachers were so supportive. I was being told daily how well I was doing. They would help me to improve with compliments and I couldn't believe how driven I had

become. I was improving in front of my own

two eyes and it was making me work even

harder. I balanced going to school and

teaching dance and I took on teaching acting

classes as well. I was literally going night and

day. It was never a struggle because I was

living my dream.

It was an incredible time in my life. I remember

having a break one night at my home studio

and asking my teacher if I could join in on her

class. This was about 5 months into my

college year. At the end of class she put her

arm around me and said "Why didn't you ever

dance like that when you were here?" and I

looked her in the eyes and said "because I never believed I could". So many times, my story could have changed. My parents could have put their foot down and ignored my pleas to stay at that studio and moved me somewhere else.

I could have easily crumbled in that toxic environment and quit but I didn't. My love and passion were too strong. I have so many wonderful memories from my time as a competitive dancer. So many amazing friends and experiences and I could write a whole book about those, but I do have to think harder to recall those memories than I have ever had to think about the bad ones. They have been imprinted in my mind and are always right there. This is the power of words. You can hear a thousand positive compliments but it is that one negative comment that will stick. As an adult, with all the tools to diffuse the impact, I still struggle at times with those negative comments.

As a child, I had no way of fighting back, no resilience. I shouldn't have had to in that environment. With my Christian upbringing and focus on the Golden Rule "Do unto others as you would have done to you" and the experiences I encountered, I became the teacher that I am today. I can't say for sure that I wouldn't still be this teacher but I do know that these experiences made me consciously aware, made me more empathetic and far more compassionate.

POSITIVE SELF-TALK

My story brings me to share that without confidence, children cannot meet their maximum potential. Words are POWER and as educators, and even as parents, we need to use them with such care and thought.

I have three areas that I have focused on and have seen amazing results in the classroom and on the stage; positive self-talk, affirmations, and "your 3 words".

POSITIVE SELF-TALK.

Studies have linked negative self-talk with lower self-esteem and higher levels of stress. Negative self-talk is an inner dialogue you have with yourself that limits your capability to reach your potential because of a disbelief in yourself and your abilities.

Negative self-talk comes in the form of limited thinking, perfectionism, feelings of depression and relationship challenges. This is why positive self-talk is a rule in my classroom. Positive self-talk has incredible benefits that include an increase in self-esteem and self-confidence, it promotes optimistic thinking, which decreases the chances of suffering from depression, it improves your performance and it eliminates stress. My students know that the word "can't" has no admittance in my class. They call it a "potty word". Whenever a student uses the words "I can't" in a sentence I immediately make them rephrase the sentence.

Yes, this does at times come with an eye roll or an exaggerated exhale, but I remind them that we listen to the words we speak and that our inner dialogue is more powerful than anything anyone will ever say to us. I help them to rephrase their sentence to "I can't do this yet but....." and they have to fill in the blank with an action plan. Here is an example of how one might finish the sentence "Miss Kelly I can't do this yet, but if I practice, and ask for help I will be able to do this soon."

I make them repeat it to me, and then we move on. This is a practice I have had in place for a long time and when I first implemented it I was surprised how quickly the atmosphere in the classroom changed.

Now, for the most part, my students just simply jump to the finished product "Miss Kelly I am having trouble with this step can you please help me?' or "Miss Kelly, I have been working on this step and I am feeling frustrated because I don't know why I am still struggling. Can you please help?"

When I catch a student using negative self-talk such as "I'm no good at this" or "I can't turn" or "I can't jump" for example, I will make them say it out loud. Then I ask them to turn to a friend and tell their friend the same thing and speak to them the same way. Almost every single student will tell me that they cannot speak to their friend that way. When I ask why, they say because it is mean.

Believe me! My hand is raised high and I am guilty of this practice of negative self-talk in my lifetime. I still catch myself at times being unkind to me. We have to teach our students

and children that WE are our own best friend.

If we would not talk to another person that way,

then we must not speak to ourselves in such a

way. I encourage them to be more consciously

aware of their inner dialogue and to change it

whenever they notice themselves being

negative.

We need to lift ourselves up the same way we

lift others. When you allow your classroom or

home to be a space where students and

children can feel confident to commend

themselves we slowly change their inner voice.

I see me students celebrating their successes

so much more and having the confidence to be proud of their accomplishments. Miss Kelly! I did it!" I always back these up with things like "Yes! You did! You were smart, you were patience, you were consistent and you worked hard. You deserve this!" with a high five.

AFFIRMATIONS

Affirmations are powerful statements that you say to yourself. You affirm to yourself whatever it is you want to happen. The act of repeating affirmations motivates, inspires and programs the mind to act in accordance to what is being said.

Affirmations help to focus the mind on the goal. The process starts with the conscious mind and then the sub conscious takes over. I have my students pick 1-3 affirmations that are not too long. They must be placed in present tense and if they are goal oriented then they are spoken as if the goal has already been attained. For example, "I am flexible and strong"; "I am courageous"; "I am powerful"; "I am creative"; "I can do all of my splits", etc.

These affirmations need to be repeated many times a day. I give them the goal of 400 times per day, which seems like a lot but in a 5 to 10-minute period you can speak that short affirmation many times. Sitting in the car, brushing their teeth or walking to school are all great times to repeat their affirmations. I really encourage them to stand in front of a mirror when they first wake up or go to bed and look themselves in the eye.

When you see yourself in the mirror and say your affirmations out loud it has an even more powerful affect. It is important to teach them that they must mean what they say and pay attention to what they are saying. It is ideal for them to be relaxed, to really believe what they are speaking and to feel the desire to have it become truth.

YOUR 3 WORDS "Your 3" is a term I coined one day when I was teaching a class of 8-11 year olds. I was struggling with this particular group of children to encourage them to be self-motivated.

They would give me the results I was looking for if there was a reward or if I got stern with them but this is not the kind of atmosphere I wanted. So, I asked them "What are the 3 words you would want someone to describe you as when speaking about you?"

Mine are Engaging, World-Class and Compassionate. I keep these three words at the forefront of my mine during every interaction I have with someone. When I am not around and people are speaking about me, I want these three words to come up in the conversation as descriptive words. I ask my students to come up with their 3 words, also.

Anyone of my students can rhyme off their 3 words when asked. When we are in class I can quickly use this as a reference for self-evaluation. "Are you being your 3 words?" If not, what are you going to do to be those things?"

Their performance changes immediately without offering a reward or raising my voice. I am able to keep the class moving, they push harder, which moves them closer to their goals and in the end results in success. This is an incredible accountability tool and it also goes hand in hand with their affirmations and positive self-talk. It is important for us as educators and parents to be conscious of the impact we have on these young, impressionable and delicate humans.

One negative comment can have a lasting effect on them that they may hold on to as their truth and have difficulty or never be able to grow past it. I know now that building my students up is just as important as the material and lessons I am teaching. Providing them with the tools to remain positive, driven, focused and goal oriented has been the proven

way to create the most successful, caring and

loving learning environment.

Homeschooling

When Homeschooling Became My Life—Insight for Teachers & Parents

By Nina Luchka

She just doesn't look happy anymore. Why does my little girl look so sad? This is not her character. What is happening at school? Maybe there's something going on and she's not telling me.

These are the thoughts that went through my head and I was steadily asking myself these questions. My daughter is a very outgoing little girl. She has got a lot of spunk and is a happy, joking kid. But I started to see changes at the end of senior kindergarten. So, grade one, I decided to homeschool her.

Grade two came and I decided to put her back in school, as she was eager to go to school and she did enjoy it. However, as the year went on I started to see character changes again. Her sparkle wasn't so sparkly. Her glow was dull. Was my little girl just going through a change now? Maybe kids' characters change as they get older? I have no idea. Unfortunately, my daughter, or any child, just doesn't come with a manual.

As I would drop her off at school, I noticed that she would go from joking around and laughing, to straight-faced, shoulders rounded and slightly hunched, every time I put her knapsack on. And she wouldn't say much as she walked away. She just wasn't the same person. This bothered me and I couldn't ignore it.

I started with just googling information and reading a ton. I came across several pieces of information on how kids are very creative and love to learn. This creativity and love for learning is squashed with the forced education. The forced, one-way-to-learn for everyone doesn't work because not every child learns the same way. They are encouraged to work for gold stars, for A's on report cards etc. Then there are the tests in class, the testing at certain grade levels. So much stress. I was never good at tests…the stress of it made me nervous and I would forget everything.

I remember grade nine, I studied hard! I failed math and so I went to summer school so I wouldn't be a year behind. The teacher pulled me out in the hallway half way through summer school and asked what I was doing there.

Looking confused I answered "Im in summer school because I failed math." He replied,

"You KNOW your math. Your marks are 90's".

Not only did I fail Math for the year, but going into grade 9 was stressful. People were telling me high school was tough. "It's WAY different than grade school."

So, I went in to high school on a mission. And when exam time came, I was ready because I STUDIED HARD! I started to study about a month and a half before exams. Everyday. I had my brothers and my dad help me. I knew my stuff. Then exams came. I choked. Totally bombed. I failed EVERY SINGLE EXAM. I tried SO hard.

I poured my heart into it and I failed. That damaged me. It damaged my ego. From that day forward, I never tried in school again. As long as I got a 50%, I was happy. I wasn't going to bust my butt, to get 90%, studying everyday THINKING I know my stuff. Those exams, made me feel stupid.

Every time exam time came, it was a hit. A hit so hard of "you're so stupid". I was embarrassed of my marks all through high school. My friends all got excellent grades. I guess I was the dumb one. THIS is how I felt being in the school system. My light did not shine bright through those years. I hated school. Absolutely hated it. Besides the sports and Phys Ed class.

I often thought though why I did so well at summer school, to have the teacher pull me aside during class to ask why I was there and that I KNOW my math. I didn't clue in until I had kids. When My first born went to school and I would tell her, "it doesn't matter WHAT mark you get. That mark does not reflect YOU, or mean you are smart, smarter than others, stupid or dumb. It just shows us where you need help, or maybe that we need to explain things differently so that you understand".

And THAT'S where the school system fails. Most teachers teach one way and that's it. Well, not everyone learns the same way. This is something I told my daughter over and over. I NEVER wanted her to think she was stupid because she didn't understand something or scored low on a test.

Not every subject will be their thing. Maybe drama, music, the arts is where the child's heart is. Maybe it's math, or science. Each child is different and will excel in that area.

Take for example, Lisa Nicolas, a motivational speaker. In English class she failed. Her English teacher went on to tell her in front of the whole class "Lisa, you have to be the weakest writer I have ever met in my entire life." Her Speech teacher said, after giving her a D- in speech, "Ms. Nichols, I recommend you never speak in public, that you get a desk job". She went on to become an International Motivational Speaker and Best-selling Author who has written 7 books.

If she would have listened to her teachers, she wouldn't be who she truly is and her passion wouldn't be able to shine and change lives. But what about kids who soak up any comments like that and NEVER try to pursue that journey because they were told they were no good at it? It's sad. We would have an abundance of passionate adults, changing the world.

When my daughter started senior kindergarten (I never sent her to junior kindergarten), I noticed how school bothered me. It bothered me when she was sitting in a class most of the day, and I was outside with my 2-year old. My son and I would be playing and enjoying the outdoors, whole my daughter was inside, sitting there, learning all day.

Sure, they get a break in the morning and afternoon for 15 minutes, and a lunch break, but was that enough? To me, it wasn't. I spend most my time outdoors with the kids. We explore, go for walks, etc. and she was inside most of the day. It didn't feel right inside me. She's a kid. She's 5.

I thought to myself, "She will be starting grade one, now they really sit and learn all day." And this hit me even more. Beautiful days, why can't they sit outside and learn. Ugh, it was tearing me apart inside that she would be cooped up all day.

I started researching kids and characters. I then came across homeschooling. Well what was homeschooling all about anyways. I searched and searched info in this. I then came across a TedX Talk by Logan Laplante, a

13-year old boy who talks about how he was homeschooled. He's a Lifehacker. Excellent talk and it spoke to me. THIS is what I wanted for my kids. THIS is how I feel kids should be raised.

So, I decided to keep my daughter home and try this homeschooling thing for grade one. How hard could it be right? It's grade one!

Yeah, it was tough. It was tough on me because you are kind of in this thing alone. There is a lot of support of other moms, but when you are at home teaching your child, its one on one. Unless you are a teacher and very confident, then homeschooling can play on you in the beginning. Every day, I ask myself, "are we doing enough work? Is she learning like she should be? Is she ahead of the game or behind? "and the big one-- "If she's behind and this all fails, it's MY fault".

All these things played on my mind. Daily. I'm not a teacher. My grades were awful in school. When it came to school I was "stupid" remember. I had some good support from some moms in the homeschooling community.

Telling me the first year is always the hardest and to just stick it out. I couldn't. I just couldn't. I ended up sending my daughter back to school for the second half of the year. So, right after Christmas she started back. She loved it! But she also Loved being homeschooled.

She did fine and I taught her well in the first half of the year, so it was easy for her to go back. As the rest of the year went by, it wasn't until the very end that I saw my daughter start to change. Just subtle changes. I just thought "well maybe this is how kids are supposed to change. Maybe this is them getting older". I didn't know. I would ask her how school was and she said it was good. She enjoys being with her friends. I would then ask her "who did you play with today?". As the year went on and I would ask her at least a couple times a week (being curious and investigating), she would say "no one. It's hard to play with someone on the monkey bars". That went on for a while.

A couple months later, as her character started to change more, it a way that just wasn't her bubbly self, I asked her "is something going on at school? Are kids being mean to you? Do you like your teacher?". I didn't know what the problem was but I could clearly see a change in her. A change that I didn't like. A change that I didn't want for her. Well, she broke down crying the one day I picked her up.

Her "friends" don't really play with her. Her "best friend" would tell the other friends not to play with her.

I get it, this is school. But she's stuck there every day with these kids. I now have to teach her and give her the tools to build up her confidence and how to respond when there's a not so nice situation. Think of it this way, which is the same scenario a child is in.

School and work are similar. You are in an office or factory, with co-workers, all day from 9-5. Everyday. Weekends off. You kind of make friends (more like acquaintances) and you are stuck there day in and day out, forcing you to engage with these people whether you like them or not, whether you get a long or not. And if there's a situation, an ongoing situation, that's stressful!

Even some adults don't know how to deal with situations like this. School is JUST the same an adult working in an office or factory.
Grade two came and I decided to keep her in school, she was eager to go to school and she did enjoy it. As the year went on this is the character I started to see again. Her sparkle wasn't so sparkly. Her glow was dull. Was my little girl just going through a change now?

Maybe kids' characters change as they get older? I have no idea...unfortunately my daughter, or any child, just doesn't come with a manual.

As I drop her off at school, she went from joking around and laughing, to straight face, shoulders rounded and slightly hunched, every time I put her knapsack on. She wouldn't say much as she walked away. She just wasn't the same person. This bothered me.

The more I looked into it the more I didn't want my child(ren) to shut down. Not that it's intentional by any means. School is a system, a set of rules; sit down, ask to get up, ask to go to the bathroom, raise your hand, you're hungry, too bad you have to wait. And then the grading… that alone can affect your self-esteem.

Wikipedia definition of Homeschooling is homeschooling, also known as home education is the education of children at home or a variety of other places. Home education is usually conducted by a parent or tutor or online teacher. Many families use less formal ways of educating.

There are different forms of homeschooling. There's unschooling, homeschooling, wild schooling, and then there are different methods of homeschooling. There's classical homeschooling, unit studies, Charlotte Manson Method, Moore Formula, Waldorf, Computer-Based, Eclectic, and textbook homeschooling. It was all overwhelming for me. I wanted to jump in and start homeschooling, but lacked the confidence and where to start.

I went on Facebook to see if there were any homeschooling pages...I found a TON! I started to join as many homeschooling pages that were in Ontario, as I could. Then I came across a local page, PERFECT! Right in my area! I contacted the person in charge of the page...to find out that she had just bought a house 4 houses down from mine. She came over and went over a bunch of things. She guided me and made me confident that I could do this. So, I decided to homeschool my daughter when she was to start grade 1.

I have to say, it was a tough decision. I'm not a teacher by any means. I don't know how to teach school. Was I even going to teach like a school. That's what I didn't want and why I chose to homeschool. Now it was me getting use to erasing what ive been taught. What society has been taught.

GO TO SCHOOL. Everyone goes to school to sit in a class all day and learn.

I didn't want that. So how was I going to teach my little girl?

In the homeschooling community I asked some of the moms how they taught. Everyone was different. Some taught A LOT, some taught a medium amount and some very little. The very little homeschooling moms would remind me "your child will guide you on what they want to learn. Follow their interests."

Well, that was even hard for me to understand. I was just over-analyzing everything…making something that was so simple, into a BIG HUGE ORDEAL.

The first year we tried, I schooled her for half a year and then sent her back. She wanted to go back as she LOVES being with people. Then the following year I kept her in school for the full year.

I also put my 4-year old in Junior Kindergarten only to take him out a month later. He wasn't ready and I wasn't going to push him to go and have him in tears. Plus, he's 4! Gheez...in Finland kids don't start school until they are 7!

The next year I kept both Kids home and decided to give it another go.
It's tough. Let's just say you fail as a teacher. All eyes and blame are on

you! When a child goes to school and the child "fails", it's the teacher's fault. So, this in itself can be very hard on the ego. Homeschooling (or not homeschooling), you have a life to take care of. You have to make sure they're well educated, they comprehend things, understand things, etc.

It can be extremely stressful and overwhelming. How do we know we are doing the right things for our child?
being a homeschooling mom can be tough.

For me, it's challenging. I've got 4 kids, aged 9, 6, 4, and 2. I have my 9-year old set up to do some work, then I help my 6-year old with sight words and math, while my 4-year old

follows what we are doing, because he wants

to do whatever his big brother (the 6-year old)

is doing. And my 2-year old is a hit and

miss. He could be playing nicely, or whining

and crying at my feet. So, most times its

challenging. I'm fortunate that my kids do

catch on fast.

We don't spend all day on schooling. Learning

is an ongoing process. In the beginning I didn't

realize I was constantly teaching them

throughout the day. But I love to explain things

and how things work. We spend about an hour

on actual sit down work with curriculum,

learning math, reading, writing and even

cursive writing (something that is not taught in schools anymore because technology is taking over). We do fun experiments, explore outside (bugs, birds, clouds, trees, flowers, vegetable garden, etc.), do crafts, build with tools, sew, bake, cook, etc. All fun things. They play a lot and we have gatherings to the museums, farms, etc. with other homeschoolers.

Having my daughter home now, I've seen her character come back. That unique, quirky, clowning around, outgoing girl is back. I have not seen the old Aspen going to school look. That's gone. It took a bit but time healed.

Earlier I mentioned that school is much like a job. The child goes to school (work), works all day with a break in the morning, lunch break and afternoon break, with the same kids every day, forcing them to choose their friends there. With adults and work, most adults don't have friends at work. Work is work. They have friends outside of work.

Some adults hate their job, and have nothing in common with people at work. How do you think a child feels? They are forced to make friends at school. Sure some friends become really great matches and they just stick. Most of the time, not so much. My Best Friend was actually my neighbor. He and I went to school and we would play with different kids there, but I didn't have as much fun with the kids at school as I did with my Best Friend that lived next door. My kids have asked me who my best friend was growing up, and it was Gordie! From birth to grade 8. He was my buddy!. It wasn't school kids.

So, when you look at the similarities of school and work, it's kind of sad to see that really we are putting our kids to work at the age of 4. Kindergarten is like a preparation for actual office work that starts in grade 1. Grade one you are to sit in your desk. You have to ask if you can do anything. I started to look into this. Wondering why school was here. Who created it and how long ago. For what purpose was school?

If you research and dig to find the true reasoning for school you will find that it is to instill discipline, not to foster learning.

Education was more about forming behavioral habits. To sit for long hours in a day. To listen and be told what to do. It's about learning how to learn, how to conform.

When I found this information, it totally made sense to me. I can see that 100%. What happens when we are adults and ready to work? We understand now how to sit for long hours and do repetitive work, day in day out. We get 2 breaks and a lunch break. Interesting. we have been taught this since grade 1.

Children are born with greatness. Every single one of them. Where did that greatness go? They are tiny, creative beings. Did you know that children, up until the age of four, are actually operating at a genius level? Pretty incredible! Really, it's amazing. And I had NO idea.

As we age we start to lose this brilliance. So at age late 20's early 30's, only 2% operate at a genius level. So Where did it go?   Now look back at what I wrote, we are sent to school to be told to sit all day, read this read that, no talking, put your hand up to be spoken to etc. And how many times is a child told "you CAN'T do this", "you CAN'T do that".

I listened to a Simon T. Bailey talk called *Listen*. He speaks about how a child will hear the word "NO" 150,000 times by the age of 17, and the word "yes" 5000 times. He continues, "the more that you hear what you can't do, where you can't go, who you can't become, there is a neurological path that is created in the brain that causes individuals to shut down."

This just speaks to me on so many levels. This talk just confirms all the more that what I'm doing for my kids, even though it can take a toll on me at times, is the right thing. The right thing for me and for them.

So, my homeschooling journey is not one that is planned and laid out daily. It's learning as we go. Yes, I teach my kids the basics of math, reading and writing, and where they should be for their grade, but we explore and research. I have them lead the way. What interests them, not me.

My goal is to keep their inner light shining bright, not dim it. To show them the strong person they are, and not hide inside—To never

listen to anyone that tells them to "tone it down

a bit."

Here's a quote, it's an absolute favorite of

mine. I've taught this quote to my kids, and

part of it hangs on my wall to read daily.

"Our deepest fear is not that we are inadequate. Our deepest fear in that we are powerful beyond measure. It is our Light, not our Darkness, that most frightens us. We ask ourselves, who am I to be brilliant, gorgeous, talented, fabulous? Actually, who are you not to be? You are a child of God. You're playing small does not serve the World. There is nothing enlightening about shrinking so that other people won't feel unsure around you. We were born to make manifest the glory of God that is within us. It is not just in some of us; it is in everyone. As we let our own Light shine, we consciously give other people permission to do the same. As we are liberated from our own fear, our presence automatically liberates others." –By Marianne Williamson

How beautiful is that quote?! I never want my

child's light inside to be turned down,

squashed, etc. And this is why I homeschool. At least until they are at a good strong age to let any kind of teaching, words, comments, to bounce right off them. This is just one reason why I choose to homeschool.

There are many reasons for parents to homeschool their children. And each reason is good for them and works for them.

It's tough being a homeschooling mom. You don't know what the future holds for your child. Which direction they will go. Or maybe we do. We are just automatically thinking from our situation, when we graduated from high school. Many of us not knowing what we wanted to do and others being pushed or

persuaded into a career. It makes me wonder

why it's said that in a person's lifetime they will

change careers 5-7 times, with 30% of the total

workforce changing jobs every 12 months.

So, maybe our light was dimmed, and not

shining as bright as it should, so our level of

genius has now diminished and we listen to

others on what we should do for our careers,

never liking our job. Believing that "this is how

being an adult and careers should be". When

in reality, true reality, our light was buried, not

letting our true self leading the way on the

journey. And years later, career after career,

job after job, more courses, you finally find your

passion and you try hard to spark that light again.

That light, that once was deep inside, is still there. Waiting for you to make it great once again. Freeing yourself from the mask that is not YOU. Freeing yourself from years of being told what to do, what not to do, how to act, how to play, how to sit, etc. Instead of just having a little guidance, and free to explore.

Explore what is curious to YOU, not to someone else. Teach our kids the same. They all have a beautiful, bright shining light inside them. A creative one. A purposeful one! Their light is needed in this world and it's such a special light that no one else has. Could you imagine a world of passionate,

creative, purposeful people? Beautiful!

Cultural Sensitivity

The Value of Cultural Sensitivity Training

By Dr. Juanita Woodson

""I want to be a doctor or a lawyer when I grow up!"

T hat is what I told my 4th grade teacher when she asked the class what they wanted to be when they grew up. Although I was young and did not have a clue how difficult or challenging it would be to pursue either of those career options, I felt I could do it. Even though they labeled me with an IEP and ADHD, somehow deep inside I believed that anything was possible and if I wanted it I could obtain it. Sadly, the teachers' response set the tone of my life for a very long time. She said to me, "No, you need to choose either a restaurant job or a janitor job." Can you imagine the humiliation I felt as she told my white counter parts they could actually be the president, a lawyer, a doctor and much more?

In retrospect, I believe perhaps it was because I was a low income African American student with what they called a learning disability that was the reason the teacher dismissed my dreams. I'm from the northside of a small city in

Illinois outside of Chicago and nobody expected any African American's there to succeed. We were a culture all of our own. We had our little small box houses, violent clubs, a million churches, dangerous parks and lots of neighborhood cookouts all in one place. We were black for sure, but we were northside blacks. You see, the northside where I grew up produced very few college-bound and career oriented blacks. You either hit it big and went to work for Kraft food factory or you got lucky and worked at the post office.

However, If you lived on the southside it meant your family had money with a big house and you possessed a greater chance of going to college and building a great career. We used to call them Oreos, black on the outside and white on the inside. We believed them to have made a deal to sell us out in exchange for money. It was what we were taught think and believe in our culture at the time. So the north and the south separated cultures of the same race. It is very important as educators that we take the extra step in understanding what I call a culture in a culture. Attending a training that explains one dimension of a culture is a waste of time. Educators have to like students enough to dig deeper and find the key to helping each student soar academically.

Fast forwarding to middle school, the principle

had orders from the superintendent

to administer IQ tests to all students. I would

never forget the day I was called into the

principal's office because of poor behavior and

he asked me why I didn't take school seriously.

I remembered what my elementary teacher

had told me, and I responded, "Because I'm

not smart". He looked at me in disbelief

and begin to shuffle through some papers on

his desk. He pulled out and showed me the IQ

test results from the one we had taken.

He looked at me and said, "Look at this, you

are extremely above average." I had scored

higher than the top honor students in the school and he proved it by showing me their results.

He told me to never let anything or anyone make me feel like I can't achieve something in life. He reinforced that my current situation could not and should not dictate my future. He strongly encouraged me to straighten up and pay attention in class because I was smart enough to do.

He also didn't feel sorry for me because I was from the northside, he just made me feel like that didn't matter. I looked at my entire life and its endless possibilities from that day forward.

Cultural Competence is the will and ability to form authentic and effective relationships across our cultural differences and differences make a difference in teaching. Culturally responsive teaching is when more students across more differences achieve higher level thinking more of the time and being present and engaged without giving up who they are.

Understanding culture does not just mean a historical study of that nationality but also the century in which we live today and the types of cultures that influence its society.

For example, the Hip Hop culture, Pop culture, LGTB community, religion and popular political stances help to shape the thoughts and

processes of the people it affects. Students are

affirmed in their cultural connections.

Students need to feel honored in their

culture and accepted. Teachers must be

personally inviting and should actually

like various cultures and accept these cultures

in order for kids to believe in them.

We need to be sure even before becoming an

educator that we like students regardless to

their race or culture. It is a good idea to be

personally inviting to each student,

by using non-threatening touches like a pat to

an arm to personally greet each one. Kids get it

when we like them. They can tell the truth from false actions.

The Classroom must be physically and culturally inviting. You need to have different nationalities of people on posters hanging on walls in class rooms. Even hang flags from all the nations of the world in an attempt to show inclusion. Spaces often reflect who resides in the spaces.

Reinforcing academic learning by catching kids being smart. Catch the moment they actually get the lesson right and affirm it immediately. We need to show that we believe in their intelligence. Instructional changes must be made to accommodate differences.

The classroom should be managed with firm consistent loving control- don't try to be just their friend, you have to have control, have a parenting type voice. Respect is key, both given and received. Competence precedes confidence.

Kids need to feel accepted, active and hands on. We must create the environment. They need to be able to take the lead in learning especially early in life before the age of 5. They are developing ways to process creativity and cortisol plays an important role and cortisol issues can cause children to block learning. They need to build learning dendrites in the brain, the need to take inert facts and figures and turn them into knowledge.

For example, many disenfranchised black boys fail in schools due to issues with learning styles and are sent to special ed. Many believe this is a new form of segregation because you can actually do all the IP requirements without labeling the child or removing him from the classroom.

By incorporating learning scenarios that speak to their life styles you can create an atmosphere of learning. Cultural competence is essential and culturally important in schools and classrooms, and it can't be learned and incorporated to provide quality education to students and their families. The ability to successfully teach students who come from cultures other than your own is call cultural competence.

It requires advancing certain personal and interpersonal cognizance and sympathies, understanding certain groups of cultural knowledge and know how, taken together, underlie effective cross-cultural teaching and culturally reactive teaching.

Cultural competence is not something that happens after taking a weekend class or training session. Educators become culturally competent over time. Culture shapes everyone both professionally and educationally.

The celebration of heroic leaders, religions, traditions, and holidays, as well as a gratefulness of the customs of different groups is what most people think culture is, it is also more than that.

Culture is an assemblage of experiences that culminate over several dynamics that include food, clothes, music, and practices.

Culture reveals who a person is and where he or she fits in the family, community, and society.

Once I watched a documentary of an urban school district who implemented a unique method of cultural diversity training to prepare new teachers for the school year. These schools were in areas where there was a high concentration of minorities.

Some schools had a large low-income Hispanic population and others had low income African American populations. Each new teacher was assigned a family to stay with for a few weeks during the summer and learn their culture. So for example, a middle class Caucasian women from a gated community far from the school district she was assigned to teach at would stay with a working class or low income African American for the summer.

Likewise, an African American teacher stayed with a Hispanic family to learn hands on about their culture. While watching this documentary I was astonished of as the family hosting project ended the teachers actually considered the host family as their real family. They had lived as a daughter or sister in the house of the host family for several weeks and was afforded the opportunity to see, hear, smell, taste, feel, and experience another culture. Surprisingly, they actually understood and enjoyed it.

I believe that most schools should implement such an awesome program similar to this one and observe how the lives of children are changed as well as how learning becomes fun and exciting for them. All it takes is a little love to make a world of difference in the learning experience of a student. One caring teacher can make the difference for a student between jail and college, the grave and a corporate career.

As for me, I did receive my doctorate degree in counseling after all. Not only did I receive it with honors but with straight A's in every subject. My very first job was a mental health therapist for a counseling program through the University of Illinois.

I actually served the population of the northside and I made a positive impact on many who remembered me and those who didn't. Not only did I become a Dr. I also became an entrepreneur, starting several corporations and I employed people from guess where, the northside. We have to keep the bigger picture in focus while educating individuals of other ethnic groups and cultural backgrounds. As an educator your mandate is or should be to enhance and enlighten the learning experience of all students in hopes of teaching them new skills. We must try harder to understand one another rather than to offend.

Only then will our communication be made clear and our intentions precise. And true respect will be reciprocated between the two. When a student feels respected and appreciated, they have no other recourse but to excel.

Each One Teach One

Effective Mentoring & Support for New Teachers

By Dr. Shekina Farr Moore

"Don't be surprised by your greatness. Be surprised that no one expected it."
–Rebecca Maizel, Infinite Days

I coach educators, school administrators and community leaders to take an unapologetic stance as they posture themselves to impact their communities and beyond. Once you know your worth, and embrace it, there is nothing you cannot do.

I often share with said clients my struggle early on as a new teacher with juggling the acronyms and paperwork, interfacing with so many personalities and even the role people's perceptions of the teaching industry played in that struggle.

A big part in overcoming my new teacher blues" crisis was having a mentor who helped me to articulate what I was experiencing in a way I could stand outside of it instead of internalizing it.

I soon came to understand that I didn't need to be understood by those outside of education, I needed to be a rock star in my classroom for my students. And before I knew it, with the help of my mentor, I was wheeling and dealing as a teacher. I soon became known as the who could relate to her students and who was professional. I had established an identity I came to love. But it wasn't done in isolation. I value the role my mentors played in my transition from novice to expert.

Approximately 40 to 50 percent of new teachers leave within the first five years of entry into teaching (Ingersoll, 2012). Nationwide, the inability to keep teachers teaching costs districts $7.3 billion a year, according to the National Commission on Teaching and America's Future (NCTAF).

These statistics are alarming. I suspect that most of the attrition stems from overwhelm and environmental factors such as lack of support.

As you move through this new world as a change agent, equally important for you as a new teacher will be to get a mentor—early. All great teachers have mentors. Relationship with a mentor only sharpens and strengthens the saw, as you will gain valuable insight beyond your education and experience.

Whether you need advice or a sounding board, a mentor can inspire and guide you, and the rewards may extend far beyond what you planned. They often include:

- Access to a support system during critical stages of your academic and/or career development
- An insider's perspective on navigating your career development
- Clearer understanding and enhancement of career or business plans
- Exposure to diverse perspectives and experiences
- Direct access to powerful resources within your profession
- Identification of skill gaps
- Greater knowledge of career success factors
- The foundation of a lasting professional network

Interestingly, you won't be the only beneficiary of the relationship. Mentors benefit as well. They (and you, as well, once you become the Mentor) build their own leadership skills by helping others to succeed and navigate their industry while grappling with life. Not only are they supporting the industry and profession, they are leaving a legacy. So, if you are afraid to seek a mentor, consider that mentors also benefit in the following ways:

- Ongoing attention to their own career development
- Exposure to the emerging talent pool
- Opportunities for recruitment to their profession
- Enhancement of coaching, leadership and management, and recruitment skills
- Exposure to diverse thoughts, styles, personalities and cultures
- The satisfaction of imparting wisdom and experience to others without a huge time commitment
- A way to give back to their association or profession
- A career network

I recommend that you seek opportunities for to observe your mentor's instruction during one block and teach the same lesson the second block. Ideally, you should meet daily or weekly and reflected on each lesson, strategies that were used to deal with classroom management issues, and the planning and implementation of the lesson.

During this time, your will be able to work alongside your mentor in order to strengthen your content knowledge, planning skills, instructional implementation, and classroom management decision-making.

Accordingly, you will have the opportunity to perform the roles and the duties of a classroom teacher. As a result of this hands-on experience, you will feel more confident to handle yourself in challenging situations, to make judgment calls based on acquired knowledge, and to deal with parents and administrators, and meet deadlines.

You will also better understand the role all stakeholders play in creating a learning environment for students. The goal is to have guided help by a mentor as you are being totally immersed in the day-to-day operation of a classroom.

Undoubtedly, as you have read, there are dilemmas and experiences that teachers must face in their careers on a daily basis. Being connected to another educator who has experiences what you will face will help you with emotional intelligence, foresight and resilience.

So, I challenge you to think of three mentors that you can reach out to with service. Yes, that's correct. How can you serve them? This is the quickest way into someone's world. Jot down their names and connect with each of them this week.

Think of 3 mentors who possess the qualities

listed below:

- Caring
- Open and honest
- Available
- Focused
- Similar goals
- Positive
- Open-minded
- Believe in you
- Experienced
- Good Character

Consider looking for a mentor that is also

outside of your immediate environment and

when you reach out to the potential mentor, be

clear in your expectations of the relationship.

Remember to be polite, tell them why, be

specific and make it easy for them. You will be

so glad you did! And you will likely desire to pay it forward in the future.

Advice for those running teacher mentoring programs

An effective teacher mentoring program should foster a strong sense of teaching efficacy and, consequently, reduce teacher attrition.

1. Make every effort to make the new teacher feel welcomed and a part of the school family.

2. Provide the new teacher with opportunities to work with an experienced and willing mentor immediately.

3. Match the new teacher with a mentor who has been carefully selected based on a record of proven success, knowledge and skills, and who is the right fit for the new teacher.

4. Provide opportunities for the new teacher to learn the ins and outs of the classroom from the start of the school year.

5. Give the new teacher a myriad of opportunities to plan and collaborate with the mentor teacher and peers as well as learn "best practices" from job embedded professional development.

6. Expose the new teacher to authentic teaching experiences and allow

opportunities for rich reflection on a daily basis.

7. Model for the new teacher how to institute a consistent and effective classroom management plan.

8. Allow the new teacher the chance to handle all types of discipline problems in order to develop an arsenal of strategies.

9. Support the new teacher as much as possible. Share valuable websites and resources.

10. Give the new teacher the opportunity to attend professional development regularly in order to grow professionally.

What Your Kids Won't Tell You

By Jessica N. Parker

I tried to be the perfect kid. I stood in the way of arguments, talked to each parent separately after the fights, I refereed in the fairest way my little being knew how, I fed my sisters, turned the TV up so the reality TV fights could outweigh our reality family fights.

I washed the dishes my dad would ask my mom to wash before he got home so he wouldn't be mad at her, I made up the best stories and told the best jokes just to prolong the peace. Unbeknownst to any other family member I didn't "crave the center of attention". I craved the pleasure of peace, ad in my child mind I had control over it.

That's where my sense of humor was developed, granted I now know that The Lord created me to be a joy bomb, but the ability to be confidently funny was surely cultivated in the cachous of my family home. Children want your unselfish love, your undivided attention and your unwavering support. PERIOD.

As a thirty-year old adult woman I am now able to speak through my child self and out of the residue of remembered experiences and tell you what your child won't to make sure you are aware of not only what they just won't say but what they would die for you to know:

I am not your husband/wife: The unfair noose we drape around the necks of our children called "support" is a doubled-edge sword. We are NOT your help meet, we are not your lover, we were never programmed to offer to you the support and love of a spouse.

We are NOT your partner in life, we are a product of it. We did not take the vows in front of God to help lift you in the ways you look for us too. YES, we as children love you as parents but there is a choice in loving you we did not make because we are not able. It is unfair to ask the product to produce something the partner is supposed to. It puts unnecessary pressure on your child to attempt to perform as your provider, safe haven, advice giver, counselor, doctor, best friend, judge and decision maker.

We know when you are unhappy: "For the kids" is an excuse parents use to make themselves feel better. I am the oldest of (3) and one thing we each knew from child is the power of prayer, you can thank my grandmother for that. So, in our best attempt to cease the chaotic chatter of our child hood home we would PRAY for my parents to get a divorce! We loved them both individually, but when the oil and water of their demeanors got together it was horrendous. We didn't care about the word "divorce" or "breakup" we just knew they were better apart.

We could of care less about having (2) parents in the home, we wanted (2) parents happy and if that meant alone, we were game for it! When parents mention that they are sticking it out for the kids, we can see your discontentment and it hurts us when you're hurt. And as a woman who was once a child, I would rather you separate and be whole apart than destroy each other wholly together.

Creatively give us what we need, stop

sheltering me: My parents knew our house was

crazy! And with that being said they were open

to offer me the structure I never knew at home.

We explored every type of art for me, which I

was and still am extremely grateful for. I took

pottery, ran track, cheered and played ball,

karate-kicked my way to first place trophies

and flipped my way to gymnast medals.

But it wasn't until I found BALLET where my

world changed. Technique and strict style was

what I needed to be disciplined and free. So

from a woman who was once a little girl I would

say get the children involved outside the

house. You never know how, by doing this, you

could be opening up a brand new world for

them as well as offering something your

current environment could never give (fully).

Setting Boundaries & Expectations

There Are No Do-over's for New Teachers

By James Mackey, IV

The first day of school is the most important day of the year. If you do not effectively establish order, it can be a long and difficult 10 months. There are no do over's. You cannot portray yourself one way on the first day of school and try and become someone else, on the second day. The students have seen the real you. As a teacher, your first goal should be to establish order, set boundaries and communicate what the expectations are inside YOUR classroom.

Students are not shareholders or business partners in YOUR classroom. Students look toward YOU as the educator to lead, guide, teach and effectively communicate with them on a day- to -day basis. They don't want nor need you to be their friend as they have plenty of those. What they do need is to see a consistent example of professionalism, leadership and an exceptional communicator who listens and is approachable while displaying a deep knowledge and passion for their subject matter. For some educators, it may take close to a year to find your *"rhythm"*. Once you find your beat, the students, your classroom, the institution and most importantly YOU, will function like a Broadway Orchestra with you as the Conductor.

Setting Boundaries

As a new, young teacher, the best career and legal advice that I can pass along to you would be to set clear boundaries with students. This is especially paramount for high school teachers, both male and female. Far too often, high school teachers in particular are caught engaging in inappropriate relationships with students. With many of those relationships untimely becoming sexual. If the educator becomes physically and or emotionally involved with a student, they can not only lose their job and jeopardize their career, but also be charged and convicted of possible statutory rape (sex with an under-age teen), depending on the state.

After studying many of these type of cases, I have found that over 70% of the educators interviewed stated that the student began to "flirt" or come-on to them, first. When this happens, the educator should immediately tell a trusted coworker.   See what he or she has to say about how to best handle this situation.

The reason why you should immediately tell a coworker is to have a witness to protect you in the event it is a "his word against her word" type of predicament. In most of those cases, the system usually believes the student. You as the educator now have an uphill battle trying to prove your innocence.

Setting clear boundaries as an educator can possibly prevent unwanted, unsolicited student attention that can attract a young teacher, thus finding themselves in a precarious position. Here is a list of what NOT to do as a teacher:

1. Never allow a student of the opposite sex to ride in your car.

2. Never exchange phone number or

   engage in text messaging

3. Never meet with a student off campus

Students' Self-Expression

A Note to Parents

By Brian Anvereen

Each year, on the first day of school, my students enter my room the same way. Apprehensive. Concerned. Unsure. But, after a week or two, after boundaries and procedures have been established, they change. They start to come into their own. Some students morph into social butterflies and vie to have one of my classroom jobs. Others realize they enjoy being off to themselves reading a book or writing. I make it my business to ensure that each of them feel safe enough to be who they are with no judgments, no consequences and no repercussions.

Does this mean I don't call on my quiet students - of course not, I do, but I also give them multiple ways to express their learning and some don't involve speaking or sharing - so they aren't always uncomfortable. I also tell my Chatty Cathys and Kevins to quiet down - but I give them the freedom to talk to through their thinking as well. I spend so much time making all my students feel like my classroom is a safe place - where they can explore who they are and what they like and every year I see it get flushed down the toilet in seconds by the one set of 'stakeholders' I cannot control.

Their parents.

Here's what happens: I'll see one of my happy-go-lucky students come in for parent conferences and stand their silently. All traces of the child I see and talk to and laugh with everyday are gone. Or one of my quiet students come in and their parents are forcing them to conduct the conference or explain something and it's very clear that they'd rather walk over hot coals. They are just there, playing whatever role they believe their parent wants to see - and losing themselves in the process.

I want to let them know I see them - that I know who they are and that this isn't them. I want to ask, "Where's my happy student?" or "What did you draw today?" or "How's that book? I noticed you've been reading it for a few days." But they just stand there, nod, and stay quiet waiting for the entire ordeal to be over. It's heartbreaking - especially after working so hard to ensure my classroom is a safe space for them.

Here's what your student isn't telling you - school is usually the one place they can truly be themselves.

We don't go home with our students but they often bring home to us each morning. Some are responsible for taking care of their siblings, some are caretakers of their parents, some don't know when, where, or how their basic needs will be met - but every morning they can come into our classrooms and shed those burdens.

They get to be themselves. Their happy, quiet, chatty, creative, and child-like selves without worry or care. Students can be who THEY are at school. They can explore their personality, make friends, make-up and break-up alliances and learn how to problem solve on their own terms. Kids need a place to be kids - and school is the one place where that can really happen.

So take a step back, relax, and get to know your student as a person - not just the reflection of yourself you want to see. See your student as the quiet creative. See your baby as the voice that others can rally around. See that child as the future - not the future *you*. Your student isn't telling you they don't love you when they don't take on your traits - they are telling you that they love themselves. It's your

job to be sure you listen.

The Expectation of Education

A Parent's Role

By Gracia C. Rich

What do we expect from our child's education? As a parent we have a clear expectation of the level of education that we want our children to receive. We expect that each day they go to school they should return home with a greater understanding of the subjects that they are taught until they become proficient in them. I think that is a cut and dried definition. But if you have ever spent any time at your child's school or with their teacher, you understand that this is not what happens. It is actually so much more. As a parent we tend to expect so much from teachers, but we need to expect just as much, if not more from ourselves.

I, myself, am not a teacher. I am just a person who has worked with teachers before, is a friend of teachers and have pretty much been around them and the education system all my life. Along with that, I was also my children's first teacher. This was something that was instilled in me by the way that I was raised. My parents too, were my first teachers. They did not wait for the schools to educate me. They started before I even entered school. I repeated this cycle with my own children. I taught them to read, to spell, to do math before they entered school the first day because I was responsible for the students they were to become. I feel that this is a lost art.

Many parents believe that it is up to teachers to educate their children. Where that is true, teachers are not the only people who are responsible for that. We have a responsibility, truthfully THE RESPONSIBILITY, to make sure that our children are properly educated to prepare them for what they will face in this world. Teachers are there to nurture, mold and build on the foundation that we have set. They water the seed, but we as parents have to plant it.

In making the transition from student to parent I have become aware of many things. The first being that a teacher's job is not just about teaching. Many teachers I know are surrogate parents, therapists, counselors and friends to all of their students. Some of these things they were prepared for, most of them they were not.

I feel that as parents we sometimes forget that our child is not their teacher's only student or priority. They have several. That is why it is best to make sure that we send our students to school with some level of understanding. If a teacher has a class of 20 or more students, how much one on one attention do you think they have for each child?

The answer is not nearly enough. That is where we as parents have to do our part. We have to give the teachers something to work with. And not only that, we have to set examples for our children. We need to talk to them about education and explain to them the important part it plays in our lives. We can't leave that up to the teachers.

The second thing I've become aware of is the giving nature of teachers. Education is not like it was when we were going to school. I remember when parents just paid a supply fee and that took care of our needs as a student for the year. Not so, in this time. I hear parents complain all the time about the supply list of items needed that are made during the summer for your child to bring at the beginning of the year.

I know it may seem excessive to many, but the truth of the matter is the supply list is just the bare minimum. Most teachers spend so much money out of pocket each year to take care of their classroom needs. As parents, we don't think too much about that. Teachers who care about the level of education that they give to their students will always go the extra mile. They will make the sacrifice needed to make sure that our children get the education they not only need but deserve. I'm certain that is more important to you than items on a list.

My third and final observation is that teachers, for the most part, are doing their best. Don't get me wrong, I know that there are some who are over it. Some who have given up on our children and the education process, but they are in the minority.

I am fortunate enough to have been around teachers who 1) love teaching and 2) love young people and want to see them excel. My daughter is one of those teachers. These are the people who make the best teachers. These are the teachers who touch and change lives. The kind that you remember for years and years.

Believe it or not, there are a lot of them still out there and we get more and more new teachers in this Nation on a day to day basis. They are looking to transform the minds of the future.

I feel that it is our jobs as parents to help our teachers as best we can. They need not only our help, but also our encouragement. They need to know when we think they are doing a good job, and more importantly when we they aren't. Most teachers love feedback and if you have some ideas on how to make the classroom experience better for your child you should tell them.

We should uplift our teachers, but also hold them accountable. But we should not set standards for them that we have not set for ourselves. It is paramount that we do our part. The parent-teacher connection makes all the difference in your child's education.

Meet the Experts

Dr. Shekina Farr Moore

Dr. Shekina Farr Moore is a scholar, a thought leader and the visionary behind the <u>Your Child My Student</u> Anthology.

Named among Atlanta's Power 25, Dr. Shekina Farr Moore, Ed.D, is an Author, Gender Advocate, Master Certified Coach (MCC) and **FORBES Coaches Council** Member.

She is also Co-CEO of Eroom Marketing Group, an empowerment parent company that oversees Intercontinental Coaching Institute, Fierce Academy, Literacy Moguls Publishing, Black Reins Magazine (the first and only black cowboy magazine in the southeast), Formidable Woman Magazine, ZOOM CON (featured on the White House's *United State of Women* in 2016) and her Non-profit, B2F Girls Worldwide--a gender empowerment incubator that offers a comprehensive certification and accreditation program and produces advocacy initiatives, campaigns and events.

She has spoken out against gender oppression and disempowerment since 1992, penning her first published article, "Blocking Out the Gender Gap", while a high school student. This article garnered the attention of the National Press for Women. She is also the author of eighteen empowerment books including: Blah to Fierce: Women's 30-Day Guide to Getting Unstuck; Beautiful, Big-boned and Brown; Black Girls Hear: Untold Stories of the Marginalized, Unsafe & Unwelcomed; and co-author of When Dark Chocolate is Bittersweet: Controversy Within A Culture.

Dr. Moore has received many national and community awards for her work with social justice and gender advocacy, including the **Volunteer Service Award signed by President Barack Obama** and a standing ovation and resolution by the GA House of Representatives.

In 2016 and 2017, Dr. Moore was named among **Atlanta's "Who's Who"** and **Atlanta's "Power 25"**, and was recognized as one of "**52 Empowering Women Who Empower Girls**" in 2014. She has been featured for her work in gender advocacy by many publications, including **Forbes, Black Enterprise, The Huffington Post, SHEEN, Rolling Out,** Millennial Mom, Courageous Woman, Today's Purpose Woman, Connected Woman, Head2Toe and more.

Dr. Moore received her B.A. in French (1999) and her M.S.A. in School Administration from North Carolina Central University (2004). She earned her Ed.S. (2009) and her Ed.D. (2016) in Educational Administration and Supervision from North Carolina State University.

Her research focused on the perspectives of Black male teachers and the recruitment strategies employed by colleges, universities and local education agencies. This garnered the attention of many, including The Twenty-sixth International Learners Conference 2019 and The National Conference on Education where Dr. Moore was asked by the School Superintendent's Association (AASA) to present her data to and lead discourse with state superintendents from around the country.

Dr. Moore is a member of Lean In Atlanta, the National Association for Multicultural Education and the National Association of Professional Women. She resides in Atlanta, GA with her husband and two children.

Leading regular live "**Candid Conversations**" teaching segments and a support group for women, her **Fierce to Formidable** movement is empowering women to *unbecome* everything that is not really them.

She enjoys family time, cooking, and binge-reading with a good, hot green tea and sushi.

For booking Inquiries, contact:
info@B2Fgirls.org.
www.shekinamoore.com | www.B2Fgirls.org

Kelly Gifford

Kelly Gifford is an early childhood educator, dance teacher, life and youth empowerment coach, business owner, author and mother.

 She has been teaching and inspiring youth for 25 years. After completing her dance training, she continued her post-secondary studies in performing arts at Randolph School of the Arts. After that, she decided to further her education and extend her love of dance and performance to younger children.

She graduated with honors as a certified Early Childhood Educator. She recently became a certified Youth Empowerment Coach with ICI because she saw a correlation between self-confidence and maximum potential and wanted to be able to provide her dancers with inspiration, goal attainment skills and the most positive environment for success. Kelly is thrilled and honored to be amongst such an incredible group of educators to bring <u>Your Child My Student</u> to you.

Jerry L. Macon

Mr. Jerry L. Macon Jr. is the founder and executive director of the faith-based, 501c3- Macon Mentor Academy and the author of the book "Solution To A Fatherless Nation."

He has been working with youth and their families for nearly thirty years with fourteen years as a public school teacher.

Mr. Macon has a bachelor's degree in social work and a master's degree in education. He is also an ordained full gospel minister, public speaker, a military veteran, certified life coach, mental health advocate and father of four beautiful and amazing children.

His passion is to help people become whom they were meant to be and with ever-increasing integrity.

To reach Mr. Macon or book any of his
services visit www.maconmentoracademy.org
or twitter @maconmentor.

Dr. Juanita Woodson

Dr. Juanita Woodson is the CEO of Impact Ministries Global, Impact Book Publishing Company, and Impact Development Foundation.

Dr. Woodson is an author, success coach, inspirational speaker, family advocate, and entrepreneur. She is an impactful apostolic and a prophetic voice with a healing and deliverance ministry who believes in the power of prophecy and prayer. She travels the world alongside her husband while taking yearly mission trips to Africa. Testimonies of breakthrough and liberation are shared by many both nationally and internationally concerning her ministry.
www.drjuanitawoodson.com

Dr. Woodson has pioneered and founded non-profit family advocate organizations that have acquired over $1.5 million in grants since 2008.

Education, training, counseling and advocacy are all necessary components of her nonprofit belief system.

Families at risk need a nest of resources to support them throughout their process. She is a mompreneur who built several businesses from home. She founded Impact Books which is a publishing company that provides self-publishers with all the tools and support services they need to be a successful author. www.impactbookco.com

Dr. Woodson has a Doctorate and Master's degree in Christian counseling from Jacksonville Theological Seminary, Bachelor's degree studies are in Psychology, Early Childhood Education, and History from Eastern Illinois University, Virginia Commonwealth University and the University of the West Indies in Cave Hill, Barbados.

Her mandate is to equip individuals to become everything God promised they could be, and to have everything God promised they could have. She believes that despite a person's past, they can still overcome and soar to new heights. Past pain can produce a powerful purpose if you choose to use it for good.

She is available for coaching, counseling, grant writing support, and speaking engagements.

Marissa Bloedoorn

Marissa Bloedoorn is the CEO of TCS Consulting. She holds a Bachelor's degree in psychology and a Master's degree in industrial-organizational (I-O) psychology.

To further her experience and expertise, she is currently in pursuit of her PhD in I-O psychology with a specialization in Executive Leadership Coaching. She recently ended her full-time position at Princeton University after eleven years by achieving her goal to completing transition into her current field in organizational development and leadership coaching.

She is a Distinguished Toastmaster, paid Professional Public Speaker, Trainer & Facilitator, Coach, Published Author, and an

Executive Board Member and consultant for multiple non-profit organizations.

As you will see today Marissa possesses a high level of energy, excitement, and insight into the importance of self-awareness as it pertains to self-development in the pursuit of personal success. She has an extensive and diverse background in corporate management, business development, and working in an Ivy League academic environment.

Marissa has been empowering professionals to think outside the box for over twenty years. Her innovative ideas and methods of discipline have been the key to her success in guiding others to reach beyond their personal limitations to maximize their performance and potential to succeed in life, career and business. Marissa's fire and passion for life are infectious, and her youthful flair enables her influence to span generations.

Marissa's current initiatives include her nonprofit organization The Bridging the Gap (BTG) Foundation, which strategizes for student success. BTG's mission is to give options to young people through leadership development, building self-confidence through training, and improving public speaking through Toastmasters International. BTG restores hope to assure students that success is within their reach.

Marissa's published work includes: The TCS Annual Magazine, "OWN IT", the following books; "OWN IT!" – A 5 Step Guide for Personal – Professional – Business Development," and "Sweetheart, Before I Say I Do," her perspective on intimate relationships, today's dating culture, and selecting your partner for life. "Maintain Your Superhero Status: A Real Parent's Perspective." Words to Inspire Books Series: In His Presence, Faith Hope & Love, Refreshed, Restored, Empowered, and Determined. And You Are the CEO of Your Life (Self-Awareness and Leadership Development book).

Stay connected on Facebook, Instagram, Tweeter, Linkedin, and BlogTalk Radio. Website: tcsconsultingllc.com

Nina Luchka

Nina is a stay-at-home, homeschooling mom of 4 beautiful, active kids ages 2,4,6,9. She chose to homeschool to show the kids more to life then what's in a textbook.

Nina is an entrepreneur guiding women to create a life and body they love, and to find their passion on this journey. Through exercise, life coaching, nutrition and holistic wellness, Nina also teaches her kids these qualities as well.

She has a strong passion to guide her kids to be who THEY want, to help them find THEIR own passions. By guiding them but also stepping back, for them to take the lead in their own journey called life.

Lisa W. Beckwith

Lisa W. Beckwith is the Founder/CEO of Lisa
Wesley Beckwith LLC. This L.I.F.E Coaching

Network thrives
to present
services
offering
individuals the
opportunity to
see themselves
mature through
executing a
healthy mindset
of self-worth—
One that
focuses on the individual, executive corporate,
and team building spectrums of life.

Lisa hopes to inspire kindness, interaction, and
active listening tactics, all while aligning
individuals' specific goals and aspirations.

Lisa is a native of Raleigh, NC. She is a
mother of four children and has one grandson.
Lisa has furthered her education through Saint
Augustine's University in Raleigh, NC,
obtaining her Bachelor's Degree in Business
Management. She is currently earning her

Master's Degree in Elementary Education at University of Southern California.

Lisa is morally driven and feels socially obligated to teach in excellence with compassion and a determined mindset. She is also a Certified Life Coach, obtaining her studies through the Intercontinental Coaching Institute (ICI) program, which establishes itself under the ICF (International Coach Federation) by-laws. Her involvement in Life coaching have given her aims to change others' lives through intervention and education, and sharing her (personal) joys of life.

This is precisely why she founded Transcendent Enrichment summer camp and tutorial program. Transcendent's mission is to partner with the community by continuing to enhance and challenge students to be the best they can be. Transcendent's motto is to teach students to Always Be Collaborating (ABC) and to make learning a fun adventure!

Lisa has been instrumental in children's education for the past five years. She is the author of a self-help/spiritual book, "Food For L.I.F.E (Lasting Impressions Forever Enjoyed)" which launched in the fall of 2018. She was inspired to write a book about L.I.F.E that identifies the disconnection that adults may have with their personal journeys due to conflicts within the stages of their lives.

L.I.F.E also teaches people how to heal from their past and create a new path for the stages left to live. Throughout her journey of helping others, Lisa has blossomed as an author. She has co-authored in a recent book, Your Child My Student Anthology, and is working on a Children's book, Summer Camp Fun with Grandson. In addition, Lisa is currently lining up projects for candle and fragrance lines, inspirations from her L.I.F.E to her audience.

Lisa's guide to life is having a Lasting Impression Forever Enjoyed (L.I.F.E) approach and to live with an optimistic mindset.

Excellence is the way!—LWB Butterfly

Shalakee Edwards-Baker

Speaking of a woman with immeasurable compassion, high-spirit, passion, love, and

hope for the human race, Shalakee Edwards-Baker comes to the limelight.

Shalakee is a licensed practical nurse and healthcare clinician with a major focus on psychology, whole body care, and patient experience. Shalakee experienced an epiphany in 2014 after traveling to Atlanta, Georgia for a weekend trip with her family. During her time here, she was drawn to the dire needs of the residents of Atlanta, only a few blocks to her hotel. She witnessed a multitude of homeless people, majorly African-

Americans of all ages. They had no shelter over their heads and protection against the elements. At this point, she realized she had to take immediate action. Warm Heartedly, she connected with these citizens and was emotionally stirred to intervene.

It was a daunting task because she encountered so many obstacles. Today, Shalakee pioneers one of the world's greatest movements, Carolinas Hierarchy of Needs, A movement to shelter the homeless and give them hope again. It aims to address chronic homelessness and educate privileged individuals on how they can play pivotal roles in transforming others out there. In March 2016, Carolinas Hierarchy of Needs (CHN) was incorporated in the state of North Carolina as a 501(c) (3) non-profit organization. She has also collaborated with both faith-based and secular organizations.

The organization went ahead to also partner with the National Black MBA Association and provided a 2-days community information panel discussion on affordable housing and home ownership and financial literacy forum. In January 2017, Shalakee actively participated as a volunteer with Charlotte Mecklenburg 2017 Point in Time Count that provided a snapshot of individuals experiencing homelessness on the night of the survey.

Shalakee's passion and expertise in the healthcare industry make it easy for her to identify with her mission. As a carrier of this great vision, she has, however, pulled together like-minded individuals to aid the execution of her vision. Presently, they serve as the Board of Directors for Carolinas Hierarchy of Needs.

With her extensive knowledge and aptness to identify the issues facing homeless communities, she has continually employed brilliant strategies to help them. Shalakee is blessed to be an embodiment of vitality to homeless people. She has a passion and desire for social activism and politics and an overwhelming desire to give back to her community. The realization of her passion spawns an unwavering drive to wake up every day and bear this cross.

Shalakee holds a Charlotte Bachelor of Science, Sociology –Social Problems and Policies, which she gained from the University of North Carolina, and Durham Technical Community College –Licensed Practical Nursing.

She is also involved with CrossRoads Reentry in her community where she teaches women currently incarcerated on important tools needed to leave behind the incarcerated life and the lifestyle which leads to incarceration, with safe and sober living and employment being critical.

"Education is the passport to the future, for tomorrow belongs to those who prepare for it today."
-Malcolm X

REFERENCES

Anderson, M., & Cardoza, K. (2016, August 31). Mental Health In Schools: A Hidden Crisis Affecting Millions Of Students. Retrieved from https://www.npr.org/sections/ed/2016/08/31/464727159/mental-health-in-schools-a-hidden-crisis-affecting-millions-of-students

Ingersoll, R. (2012). Beginning teacher induction WHAT THE DATA TELL US. *Phi Delta Kappan*, 93(8), 47-51.

National Alliance on Mental Illness (Ed.). (2018). NAMI. Retrieved November 27, 2018, from https://nami.org/Learn-More/Public-Policy/Mental-Health-in-Schools

National Alliance on Mental Illness (Ed.). (2018). NAMI. Retrieved November 27, 2018, from https://www.nami.org/learn-more/mental-health-conditions/schizophrenia

Scheid, T. L., & Brown, T. N. (Eds.). (2009). Retrieved November 25, 2018, from http://citeseerx.ist.psu.edu/viewdoc/download?doi=10.1.1.466.9749&rep=rep1&type=pdf

Stanberry, Kristin, (2014 - 2018). Understood.org USA LLC. Retrieved from https://www.understood.org/en/school-learning/special-services/ieps/5-common-misconceptions-about-ieps#slide-5

Vanderbilt University. (2018). Vanderbilt University. All
    rights reserved.Retrieved from https://iris.peabo
    dy.vanderbilt.edu/module/acc/ Vanderbilt
    University. All rights reserved.

https://www.teachthought.com/the-future-of-
learning/how-teaching-is-changing/

More Anthologies

Available on Amazon

Black Girls Hear

Letters to Our Daughters

Learn more about

Your Child My Student

at

www.B2Fgirls.org

43154193R00188

Made in the USA
Middletown, DE
22 April 2019